ADHD & Us

ADHD & Us

A Couple's Guide to Loving
and Living with Adult ADHD

Anita Robertson, LCSW

callisto
publishing
an imprint of Sourcebooks

Copyright © 2020 by Callisto Publishing LLC
Cover and internal design © 2020 by Callisto Publishing LLC
All illustrations used under license from Shutterstock.com.
Art Director: Amanda Kirk
Art Producer: Hannah Dickerson
Editor: Meera Pal and Samantha Holland
Production Editor: Jenna Dutton

Published by Callisto Publishing LLC C/O Sourcebooks LLC
P.O. Box 4410, Naperville, Illinois 60567-4410
(630) 961-3900
callistopublishing.com

Printed and bound in China.
WKT 22

♥

To my incredible, supportive husband,
Carlos, who encouraged me to write
this book because he believed it could
help others. And to my son, Nico.
I hope this book helps create a world that
embraces neurodiversity, that will in turn
enrich your life and personal relationships.

Contents

Introduction

I've always been interested in how relationships work, particularly why some relationships are fulfilling and supportive and others are not. No matter where we fall on the relationship spectrum, I believe that strengthening our primary relationship can have a positive impact on every area of our lives.

People are generally at their best and worst in intimate relationships, so doing the work can be both rewarding and challenging. In my role as a therapist, I have witnessed the healing, growth, and deepening love couples experience when they work on improving their relationship. What's more, I actively invest in my own relationship, which continues to be the best investment I've ever made. In our bicultural and bilingual relationship, my partner and I are always speaking our nonnative languages. In some ways, this has helped me in my work with neurodiverse couples—that is, couples with one partner with ADHD and one non-ADHD partner. I am very aware of how things can get lost in translation or misunderstood!

My training and experience in couples counseling has taught me that not all strategies work for everyone. In fact, some common techniques can make things worse if one partner in the relationship has ADHD. This is because many interventions are geared for non-ADHD brains. Over the years, I've come to understand that there are five "Relationship Pillars" that can help neurodiverse couples flourish. Combining these foundational pillars with a common language can make a huge difference between falling into a toxic cycle of negativity and resentment, and finding fulfillment and support in your relationship.

Early on, one neurodiverse couple I worked with couldn't understand why their amazing relationship fell into a negative cycle once they started planning their wedding. After their first session, I saw that they lacked effective communication strategies and tools. Their experience inspired me to create my ADHD Relationship Bootcamp to help neurodiverse couples build the relationship skills they need and allow the ADHD brain to thrive. Through the bootcamp, my clients were able to implement effective strategies, resolve most of their issues, and move forward with their wedding.

Preventive counseling can strengthen a relationship, especially for couples navigating ADHD. The sooner a couple begins counseling to make their relationship the best it can be, the fewer challenges and conflicts they will need to overcome. The Five Relationship Pillars create an environment where a neurodiverse couple, no matter how long they've been together, can enjoy all the benefits their neurodiversity offers while avoiding the common pain points discussed in this book. My hope is that this book helps you cultivate and nurture a loving, thriving relationship.

How to Use This Book

This book is designed to help you understand why common issues arise in neurodiverse relationships and teach you how to navigate those issues using effective strategies. The first chapter covers some of the basics of attention-deficit/hyperactivity disorder (ADHD). This information should help you better understand why the "ADHD brain" does what it does and why it needs certain strategies to function at its best. You'll also learn about the Five Relationship Pillars that you will be working on strengthening throughout the book.

The remaining chapters take a deep dive into common problems for neurodiverse couples and, using real-life examples, shares each type of partner's unique perspective. For each of the real-life examples, names and identifying information have been changed to maintain confidentiality. After reviewing how the conflict is related to ADHD or to an absence of one of the Five Relationship Pillars, you will have an opportunity to practice strategies on how to get back to a loving, healthy state, including exercises to help you master each strategy. There are activities for both partners so that each person can work toward strengthening the relationship pillars or improving executive function, which we'll discuss more later. If you like to skim books before diving in, the takeaways that conclude each chapter provide an overview of what that chapter covers.

Corresponding icons for each relationship pillar or executive function (located underneath each strategy heading) highlight what that strategy or exercise is designed to reinforce. Some strategies and exercises require a pen and notepad. Others will ask you to use objects you have around the house. Get ready to learn, grow, and have fun again!

Each partner in a neurodiverse relationship is unique, so the issues presented in this book are generalizations. You and your partner may or may not relate to some of the scenarios, or may relate to varying degrees. And although this book focuses on the negative scenarios that can occur in a neurodiverse relationship, you don't have to be stuck in a negative cycle before using these strategies. Ideally, this book can show you what to look out for and teach you to avoid common pitfalls.

This book isn't a substitute for professional treatment or support. It is intended to educate and create understanding and empathy. Over time, each of you can become fluent in your partner's language of how best to love and support them. Gaining insight into how each of you interprets events and how you invest in your relationship can help pinpoint where things may be going wrong. Most couples I meet work really hard at their relationship but still end up in conflict because they are using the wrong skill set. With this book, you will learn specific techniques that will help you better understand each other, appreciate your differences, and turn those differences into the foundation for a thriving and loving neurodiverse relationship.

CHAPTER ONE

Wired Differently

I t's not unusual for couples to face relationship challenges at some point. It's part of navigating life with another human being. When one partner has attention-deficit/hyperactivity disorder (ADHD), however, the challenges are unique. This is because they arise from differences in how the brain operates. Oftentimes, the challenges are mainly due to a lack of education concerning how ADHD can impact relationships. This chapter introduces common terms you will come across throughout the rest of the book. You'll learn some basics about adult ADHD and executive functions, and why ADHD may present more relationship challenges during certain stages of life. This chapter also introduces the Five Relationship Pillars, which will be your common language moving forward.

ADHD & YOUR RELATIONSHIP

Couples navigating any relationship often start off feeling happy, in love, and on solid ground. As time passes, they may start feeling bewildered, helpless, and frustrated, but only if they don't have the right tools to build their relationship, make it stronger, and withstand challenges. Some couples try counseling, self-help books, and/or adopting new habits and activities to strengthen their relationship. Unfortunately, such resources are often geared toward couples who aren't facing the challenges of ADHD and navigating a neurodiverse relationship. Eventually, this can leave both partners in the relationship feeling resentful toward each other. Here's an example:

> Jake and Erin began their relationship with a deep attraction and a strong admiration for each other. Erin admired Jake's creativity as a successful entrepreneur. He liked to travel, was active in sports, had several great friends, and loved making grand romantic gestures. Jake was the partner Erin had always dreamed of having.
>
> After they moved in together, their relationship began to change. At first, Erin didn't mind picking up after Jake every once in a while. She used to see it as an endearing act of care. Over time, she began to wonder why Jake just couldn't throw his tea bag away after he used it or do any number of other simple things. She began to tell herself that if Jake cared about her, he would do the things she asked him to do around the house. After all, he was able to run a business, so why couldn't he put something in the trash? Jake, on the other hand, started to get angry whenever Erin would express her frustration over what he considered unimportant. Couldn't she see how hard he was trying to be a good partner and how much he cared? Both partners began to feel deep-seated resentment and pain toward each other. The daily reminder of household responsibilities had replaced the chemistry and sense of adventure the couple once shared.

Jake and Erin were experiencing the type of miscommunication that occurs in couples when one partner has ADHD. Typical techniques that often help couples, such as explaining why it's important to have an organized house, don't result in the same behavior changes for someone with ADHD. You see, a relationship in which one partner has ADHD and the other does not is similar to having one partner who speaks only Italian and the other who speaks only French. Without a translator, it's virtually impossible to avoid misunderstandings. Even with a good translation tool, misunderstandings can still happen. All couples face conflict at some point in their relationship, even when they do speak the same language. They often turn to tried-and-true methods and techniques to strengthen their relationship and improve their communication, and as I've mentioned, the tried-and-true doesn't always hold true for neurodiverse couples.

Fortunately, there are specific solutions to help alleviate the frustration and conflict that arise in a relationship where one partner has ADHD. The rest of this book is dedicated to sharing those tools for navigating your relationship. But before we move on, let's create a foundation of knowledge about the ADHD brain. Through education, both you and your partner will better understand each other and learn to navigate your relationship.

Neurotypical versus Neurodiverse

The term "neurotypical" is used in psychology to describe someone who has typical development in cognitive, social, and physical abilities. There are still many differences from person to person with a neurotypical brain, but they tend to hit certain milestones around the same time. "Neurodiverse," meanwhile, is a term that acknowledges neurological differences in people or relationships. If someone is neurodiverse, it means their brain functions differently from the societal "norm." Autism, ADHD, and dyslexia are common examples of neurodiversity.

Relationships in which one partner has ADHD and the other does not are considered neurodiverse because each partner's brain functions in its own way. One way isn't inherently better than the other; neurodiversity can bring strength and resiliency to couples. However, there is more acceptance, knowledge, and resources for a neurotypical person, meaning that neurodiverse people may struggle more if their environment does not embrace neurodiversity. For example, without a supportive environment, children with dyslexia will typically struggle in school because classroom lessons are generally designed for neurotypical learners. However, now that there is more awareness, better testing, and early intervention for dyslexia, children can be taught in a way that works for their brain. In the same way, both partners in a neurodiverse relationship can do their part to create a healthy, supportive environment in which they both thrive.

Positive versus Negative Reinforcement

Positive reinforcement is giving someone a positive reward or incentive for certain desired behavior. For example, receiving a bonus for completing a task at work is positive reinforcement. Negative reinforcement, on the other hand, is giving someone a negative consequence for behavior that a person should try to avoid—for example, losing your job for not completing a task at work.

Notice that in both examples the goal is the same: complete a work task. There are two different ways to motivate someone to accomplish that goal. Relationships use positive and negative reinforcement all the time to influence behavior, sometimes unknowingly. A 2015 study in the journal *Behavioral and Brain Functions* found that children with ADHD have a heightened sensitivity to positive reinforcement, which increases their ability to complete tasks. Positive reinforcements, like praise, are necessary for an ADHD brain to thrive in a relationship.

ADULT ADHD

People with ADHD often handle crises well. Society needs a few people who will go toward danger when the rest of us back away. That's why a lot of people with ADHD pursue careers that involve crisis, change, and stimulation, like firefighters, ER doctors and nurses, entrepreneurs, and performers. These types of careers allow the ADHD brain to shine. People with ADHD who enter these fields often receive positive feedback on their ability to stay focused in high-pressure situations and calmly handle emergencies, whereas their neurotypical counterparts often become overwhelmed.

People with ADHD tend to be creative and great at solving problems because they're nonlinear thinkers. They can see and view things from different angles because their brains are processing a lot of information all the time. For example, someone with ADHD is likely to jump into a project and figure it out without reading the directions. In *ADDitude Magazine*, Dr. Edward Hallowell, a leading expert in ADHD, explains that ADHD brains can hyperfocus when they are interested in something, allowing for long periods of extreme productivity. We want (and need) ADHD brains in our society because they have natural abilities that neurotypical brains don't have.

Although there is still much to learn about ADHD, the following are important highlights of how the ADHD brains functions differently from neurotypical brains, based on our current understanding:

Brain differences. According to the American Academy of Child & Adolescent Psychiatry, ADHD brains differ in size and neural pathways. ADHD brains tend to have a smaller frontal lobe, which controls executive function skills like organization, self-control, and attention (more on this later).

Neurotransmitters. ADHD brains produce less dopamine and norepinephrine, which are connected to the brain's reward center. Dopamine helps the brain determine if a task is worth the effort. Lower dopamine levels mean that the reward or consequence would need to be higher for an ADHD brain to become motivated to engage in an activity.

Default mode network (DMN). The DMN is made up of parts of the brain that shut down when the brain is focused on a task in a neurotypical individual. This allows another network to turn on to help focus on the task at hand. The DMN does not shut off in ADHD brains, according to a review published in the *Yale Journal of Biology and Medicine*. This makes it harder for someone with ADHD to focus on a task because they have two competing "networks" engaged at the same time. A study published in the *Journal of Child Psychology and Psychiatry* showed that activity in the DMN decreased in ADHD brains when individuals were offered a high reward or were given medication. This explains why medication, like Ritalin, can help an

ADHD brain focus: Decreasing activity in the DMN network allows an ADHD brain to focus. More research is needed on DMN and ADHD, but this study may explain why praise from the non-ADHD partner (the high reward) can help resolve the common conflicts discussed in this book.

Genes. There is a strong genetic component for ADHD. According to Dr. Russell Barkley, an internationally recognized authority on ADHD, an estimated 75 to 80 percent of variation in the severity of ADHD results from genetic factors. If one child has ADHD, there is a 25 to 50 percent chance that a parent or sibling will also have ADHD.

As a neurodiverse couple, it's critical that you both understand there are actual differences between your brain and your partner's. Here are two main takeaways:

- Some "easy" tasks are more challenging for someone with ADHD because of how their brain operates.
- A reward, such as praise and recognition, from their non-ADHD partner will change how the ADHD brain works, making challenging tasks less difficult for them.

Keeping these two takeaways in mind will drive home the importance of learning and applying the new techniques described in this book to strengthen your neurodiverse relationship.

Why Are Adults Being Diagnosed with ADHD?

ADHD is a neurological disorder that is typically diagnosed in childhood. Symptoms often show up early in life and can persist into adulthood. Children are often diagnosed after a teacher or school counselor notices differences in their behavior and cognitive abilities compared to their peers.

Due to a lack of awareness, identification, and information in the 1980s and 1990s, today's adults with ADHD are less likely to have been diagnosed as children. According to an analysis of ADHD data published in the *Journal of the American Academy of Child & Adolescent Psychiatry*, in 1998, only 3 to 5 percent of children were diagnosed with ADHD, despite estimates of 9 to 11 percent of children being affected. Experts have improved their ability to identify and diagnose ADHD in childhood, and in 2016, Centers for Disease Control and Prevention (CDC) data shows that 9.4 percent of children were diagnosed with ADHD.

Because so many of today's adults with ADHD were probably undiagnosed as children, this population is more commonly being diagnosed later in life. Moreover, due to the high genetic link in ADHD discussed previously, many adults often receive their diagnosis after having a child diagnosed with ADHD. Another reason that adults are diagnosed later in life is because either they or their partner become aware of and recognize the symptoms of ADHD in themselves or their partners.

THE BRAIN AND ADHD

Executive functions are the cognitive abilities that enable humans to complete complex tasks. We'll go over the "Big Five" in a little while. For now, think of the group of executive functions as a command center. If things are organized, planned, and communicated effectively, tasks and goals are accomplished more efficiently. Without a strong system, things may take a lot longer to accomplish or you may see some wrecks along the way that cause major delays and frustrations.

Executive functions are both biologically based and learned through experience. Experts Dr. Peg Dawson and Dr. Richard Guare compare the development of executive functions to the development of language. We are wired to develop language skills, but those pathways need to be nourished as the brain develops for us to effectively understand and use language. In the same manner a child learns language, they develop their executive function skills with parent and teacher support. For example, toddlers are not naturally gifted at putting things away, but they have the wiring to learn to put things away. This is a skill that parents teach and reinforce throughout the child's development. Strategies for teaching skills that work for most brains won't work for ADHD, though. In fact, they can have the opposite effect, leaving kids and parents frustrated and feeling like failures.

Executive functions are necessary for "adulting"—that is, when you start to manage multiple responsibilities like finances, the home, kids, work, and so on. There are certain times when a couple needs to use more of their executive functioning skills. Here are a few examples:

- Planning a wedding
- Buying and maintaining a home
- Raising children
- Working multiple and/or demanding jobs
- Taking care of a sick parent or loved one
- Moving

Most couples normally experience some stress in their relationship during these events. However, with neurodiverse couples, these types of situations may create a toxic cycle because the couple is using the wrong tools to address conflict. The neurotypical partner can easily activate networks in their brain that make it less challenging to complete tasks in these areas. The partner with ADHD isn't able to do the same. These neurological differences lead to the common conflicts we'll discuss in later chapters.

The Criticism Filter

Because most adults with ADHD were raised in a home or school environment that didn't have the knowledge and interventions that are helpful for the ADHD brain, they most likely grew up receiving more negative messages than the average child. They were likely told they weren't trying hard enough (when they were trying really hard) or that they were careless, lazy, or forgetful. They were probably also on the receiving end of anger and frustration from the adults in their lives who didn't understand how an ADHD brain works and how to help them succeed.

In *ADDitude Magazine*, psychiatrist and ADHD expert Dr. William Dodson notes that by age 12, children with ADHD feel flawed and different because they receive an estimated 20,000 more negative messages than the neurotypical child. These formative experiences influence some of the common conflicts experienced by neurodiverse couples. From my observations, adults who received a lot of negative messages as a child will translate all feedback as criticism even though there may be nothing critical in the statement itself.

Many of my clients with ADHD can relate to the following analogy: After being involved in a car accident, most people will become hyperaware of potential danger on the road. They may see a car merging onto the highway and react as if they are in danger even though they aren't. They may quickly respond by moving into another lane to avoid the perceived threat without checking their rearview mirror. Even though this act may put them in more danger, they think they are protecting themselves. In a way, the adult with ADHD has had so many "crashes" with people they care about that they become hypervigilant to danger in the form of criticism or rejection. They start hearing criticism in casual statements and respond in an intense way in an effort to protect themselves.

This isn't an inherent trait of ADHD; it is more a product of growing up in an unfriendly ADHD environment, which unfortunately is common for many adults with ADHD today. In chapter 3, we'll go more in depth on how the criticism filter can contribute to conflicts and misunderstandings in a relationship, along with helpful strategies you can use.

ADHD "Brakes"

On his website, Dr. Edward Hallowell describes ADHD brains as powerful Ferrari engines with bicycle brakes. ADHD brains are strong at processing a lot of information, nonlinearly. They are also able to hyperfocus, allowing them to work nonstop on something that interests them. ADHD brains thrive when they are working on a creative or interesting project. However, their executive functions (the "brakes") are not as strong as they are in a neurotypical person and can get them into trouble if they don't recognize that their "brakes" are failing. Many people with ADHD respond to this analogy; it can help them challenge their criticism filter. The non-ADHD partner can also use this term to communicate with their partner. Saying "Your brakes might be failing you" would likely be well received by the ADHD brain because it isn't a personal critique of their character.

How ADHD Challenges Both Brains

ADHD can be confusing to both partners in a neurodiverse relationship. If something interests them, the partner with ADHD can hyperfocus and spend all day on a project and finish it without distractions. This can confuse their neurotypical partner, who doesn't understand how they can successfully finish complex tasks but can't do so in other areas. Here's an example:

> Marissa, who has ADHD, normally dreads tax time. She isn't a fan of entering her tax information because she often makes mistakes. This frustrates her partner, who has to take on this responsibility for her. When Marissa started a new job managing volunteers who filled out tax forms for those in need, she discovered that she really liked doing other people's taxes. This is because ADHD brains often enjoy big challenges with big rewards. Doing other people's taxes was like solving a puzzle on how to get the biggest return. Additionally, ADHD brains are fueled by praise. Because Marissa was so good at getting refunds for her clients, she was getting a lot of praise for her work. By using her hyperfocus with a helpful reward system, she was able to excel in this detail-oriented work. Her partner couldn't understand why this didn't translate to Marissa being able to help herself.

If your partner has ADHD and is successful at work or with friends but not at home, it can create tension in your relationship. It can appear as if they are choosing to disengage with you, when in reality, you both just need to know that it's a function of how their brain operates. When you understand this, you can each learn helpful skills to make things less challenging.

EXECUTIVE FUNCTIONS: THE BIG FIVE

Although there are many executive functions, let's focus on the five big ones, which are those that commonly create relationship conflicts when they aren't working as they were intended to. Whether or not someone has ADHD, they may be stronger or weaker in certain areas. In general, though, people with ADHD struggle with executive function skills across the board.

Attention

People with strong attention skills are able to stay focused until a task is done—even if it's tedious or takes sustained effort. ADHD brains generally can't filter out stimulation, so they are usually paying attention to everything at once, making it difficult to pay attention to the task at hand. This makes it challenging for someone with ADHD to finish things they start because they are easily distracted. They simply aren't wired to naturally sustain the attention needed to complete a task.

It can be frustrating when one partner is multitasking and/or can't seem to focus on what the other partner is saying. Smartphones can be a huge distraction for an ADHD brain—along with most brains, of course. Many partners may feel like the other person's phone takes priority over them, which can cause resentment. When couples embrace or gaze deeply into each other's eyes (as opposed to their smartphones!), the human brain releases the hormone oxytocin. Oxytocin is known as the bonding or love hormone; it helps people feel close and connected. If either person is distracted by random stimuli (normally the partner with ADHD) or a mess in the house (normally the non-ADHD partner), the couple loses out on moments that can strengthen their connection and relationship.

Organization and Planning

A person with strong organization and planning skills is able to plan and prioritize the steps of a task and successfully complete it. This skill is also needed to keep a house in orderly condition. Organizing and planning don't come naturally for the ADHD brain, so they tend to be weak in this area. Because their brain is focused on all the information around them, they can't figure out where to start. They may also end up focusing on one small aspect of a task without keeping the end goal in mind and thereby never reaching it. Weak executive function in this area can show up in a relationship as the inability to plan a date night, for example. The partner with ADHD may have too many ideas and have trouble knowing which to choose or where to start. For example, they may forget important ingredients they need for a special recipe and keep running back to the store, leading to a late-night dinner.

Working Memory

Working memory is the ability to remember things short term. This could be remembering what someone just said, such as their name. The ADHD brain usually has weaker working memory skills than their neurotypical counterparts. This can impact relationships when someone consistently forgets information and stories their partner has shared with them. Working memory is also important for remembering steps that are required to complete a task, like getting ready for work. This skill helps people assess how long projects or tasks will take to complete. A weak working memory can lead to being late, over-committing oneself, and forgetfulness.

Emotional Regulation

Strong emotional regulation is the ability to separate emotional input from one's behavior. People with strong emotional regulation can identify their emotions and make decisions that will be helpful to the situation instead of reacting purely based on how they feel. ADHD brains tend to feel things intensely. They are also processing more information at once so it can be overwhelming for their brains to be able to identify their emotions, which then makes it a challenge to regulate them. This can show up as intense excitement, love, and happiness, which is generally a bonus for a relationship. On the flip side, the partner with ADHD can also experience intense feelings of anger, frustration, and negative energy.

Self-Control

People with strong self-control have high-response inhibition—in other words, they can keep their impulses in check. They are able to consider long-term consequences and exhibit restraint to achieve a larger goal. For those with ADHD, exercising self-control can be a challenge, which can lead to conflict in a relationship. For example, financial concerns are a typical stressor in any relationship; however, if one partner makes impulsive purchases that take away from long-term savings due to weak self-control, this can harm the health of the relationship.

Executive Function

These skills are necessary for responsible "adulting." Because the ADHD brain naturally has weaker executive functions, or "brakes," it's no surprise that common conflicts arise in neurodiverse couples. Although there are many strategies to effectively compensate for weaker executive functions, these strategies are usually designed for the neurotypical brain, and they tend to amplify the conflict, leaving the couple even more frustrated. There's no cause for concern, though: Once you and your partner have the right tools, your relationship can thrive. For this to happen, you both need to take ownership of your relationship and discover new ways of connecting, communicating, and functioning.

▶ TIP The icon above for executive function will be seen in strategies later in the book, indicating that the strategy uses an executive functioning tip that has a higher probability of success for an individual with ADHD. (You'll also see icons for each relationship pillar later on pages 17 and 18.)

DO YOU HAVE ADHD?

If you suspect that you or your partner has ADHD, it's best to seek an evaluation from a medical professional who can help guide you on your journey. Even if you relate to some traits of ADHD, it doesn't mean you have ADHD; only a professional can diagnose you. With that said, it's helpful to be aware of what to look out for. Here are some of the more common ADHD symptoms:

→ Trouble starting projects
→ Difficulty organizing complex tasks (that don't interest them)
→ Trouble keeping appointments, being on time, or remembering obligations
→ Trouble sitting still
→ Always on the go/endless energy
→ Easily distracted; hard to focus on uninteresting tasks
→ Makes careless mistakes on homework or paperwork
→ Misplaces things at home and/or at work
→ Trouble winding down
→ Has racing thoughts and ideas
→ Talks a lot, interrupts, or blurts out responses
→ Zones out when others are talking
→ Difficulty waiting their turn
→ Difficulty sustaining attention
→ Avoids tasks that require mental effort, which they do not find interesting

Many people learn skills to cope with these traits as they age. However, if they were not introduced to effective skills for an ADHD brain, they may still struggle with these into adulthood. If you recognize yourself or your partner in these common traits, it's entirely possible you have undiagnosed ADHD. Again, it's important to seek a professional evaluation for an accurate diagnosis.

COMMON ISSUES

Conflict in a neurodiverse relationship tends to arise in situations when there is a greater need for executive function skills. Normally, this occurs after the couple is living together (not during the exciting, fun dating stage). Conflict can arise when the couple embarks on anything that requires additional responsibility, such as having a baby or getting a pet. The inability to complete necessary tasks to maintain a household can leave both partners feeling frustrated, resentful, and angry. Let's take a look at a typical conflict cycle.

1. The neurotypical brain can't understand why it's so difficult for their partner to do something they've asked, like cleaning up after themselves.

2. The partner with ADHD initially responds to the requests and may make grand gestures, like cleaning the house or finishing a project to make their partner happy. However, they may not complete the tasks or be able to sustain the day-to-day tasks their partner is asking of them.

3. Over time, the neurotypical partner tries to make sense of their partner's failure to meet these simple requests by misinterpreting it to mean that their partner does not care, love, or respect them. They find themselves constantly feeling disappointed and frustrated.

4. The partner with ADHD starts believing that their partner can't see the effort they're putting in and feels misunderstood and unappreciated.

If this cycle continues, it can become toxic. To break the cycle, the couple needs the right tools to help them communicate more effectively. Keep in mind that anyone can have stronger or weaker areas of executive function and must find appropriate workarounds. However, as mentioned, common strategies designed for neurotypical people won't work for those with ADHD. Without the right tools, both partners will end up feeling helpless and hopeless.

Let's take a look at the four areas that tend to create the most common issues in a relationship between an ADHD brain and a non-ADHD brain. While each issue corresponds to one of the five executive functions, weak emotional regulation intensifies all of these conflicts as bigger feelings and reactions when discord occurs. Being aware of these potential pain points is the first step toward exiting a negative cycle.

Weak Attention: "Never Finishes a Task"

ADHD brains light up over big, creative tasks, which shows up as excitement. It can be very contagious and inspiring to their partner. Over time, the uncompleted projects in the house may become daily reminders of their partner's inability to finish a task. This scenario can lead to feelings of frustration on both sides of the partnership. One partner is frustrated because the supplies are strewn about the house, and the other partner feels unappreciated for their efforts.

Weak Organization and Planning: "Never Starts a Task"

An attractive quality of an ADHD brain is the ability to produce many creative ideas. At first, the big dreams and projects may create feelings of excitement and a sense of connection between partners. Over time, if the ADHD brain has weak organization and planning that makes it challenging to start a task, their partner may realize that nothing actually comes from these big ideas and begins showing less interest in their partner's dreams. For the partner with ADHD, this lack of interest can lead to feeling unloved, unsupported, and frustrated.

Weak Working Memory: "Always Forgets"

A person with weak working memory forgets things such as picking up something from the store, an important anniversary, or their kid's musical performance. Over time, their partner may imagine that they simply don't care enough to complete the tasks or to be there for their family.

Weak Self-Control: "Blurts Things Out"

Someone with ADHD who lacks response inhibition may speak all their ideas and thoughts aloud as soon as they pop into their head. At first, this can make conversations more interesting and enhance the connection between partners, but over time this tends to become less endearing. The non-ADHD partner may become frustrated, annoyed, or feel disconnected if they are constantly being interrupted.

THE FIVE RELATIONSHIP PILLARS

Practicing the Five Relationship Pillars—praise, acknowledgment, games, growth mindset, and positive acceptance—can benefit all couples no matter their challenges. But with a neurodiverse couple, they create the foundation of a healthy environment for the ADHD brain, which also benefits the non-ADHD partner. When the pillars are in place, they can prevent toxic relationship patterns from developing or continuing.

Couples who master the Five Relationship Pillars see a quick decrease in the issues they commonly face in their relationship. This isn't treatment for ADHD, but it will give you helpful tools for building a strong relationship. It won't change or strengthen weak executive function skills, but it will get you out of stuck places. When these pillars motivate your interactions with each other, a supportive and fulfilling relationship is in your grasp.

🏆 Praise

Praise is fuel for an ADHD brain. It can act as a great motivator. The more praise a person with ADHD gets, the better they function. This is because receiving praise gives the ADHD brain the extra dopamine a neurotypical brain would receive just from completing a task. Praise can also decrease activity in the default mode network (page 5), making it possible to successfully complete tasks.

The amazing thing about the ADHD brain is that it will do challenging things for the right reward, and that can be something as simple as their partner's happiness and praise. Though it may be difficult to understand, a person with ADHD needs praise when they complete small, mundane tasks they find challenging. In a neurodiverse relationship, big and small celebrations need to be part of your everyday life.

👍 Acknowledgment

Each of you must acknowledge the effort and sacrifice you are both making to strengthen your relationship. Recognizing that your brains work differently is essential. A basic understanding of ADHD will help you successfully separate the ADHD symptoms from the partner with ADHD themselves.

🎲 Games

We all need time for play, novelty, and adventure with our partners, but ADHD brains are at their best when they're having fun! Chances are, the partner with ADHD likely brought this playful aspect to your relationship. Playing games and keeping things new and interesting is a must in any relationship, but without some fun and games, an ADHD brain can start to feel suffocated. The best way to keep things fresh and fun and help the partner with ADHD get things done is to turn tasks into games. Also, engaging together in fun, novel activities can help the partner with ADHD stay focused and help both partners feel more connected.

🧠 Growth Mindset

Growth mindset is a term that was coined by psychologist Carol Dweck a few decades ago. Today, this term describes the idea that we can and will continue to grow and learn throughout life because our brains are malleable. (See The Science of Neuroplasticity on page 19.) Along these lines, a relationship growth mindset is the idea that a relationship will grow and develop over time with the correct input. The focus is on the effort made; this is more important than getting it correct the first time. Every couple will experience conflict and disappointment. The difference is: Do you grow, learn, and deepen your connection because of it, or let it define your relationship?

If a couple understands that they are both growing individually and relationally, it will help them stay connected and motivated to learn more about their relationship when times are tough. The connection comes from staying curious and open to feedback on the needs of the relationship. No one is a "failure" for not knowing something about the other; it provides an opportunity for a deeper, more secure connection. Embracing your mistakes and focusing on how to overcome them will help your relationship flourish.

⊕ Positive Acceptance

Positive acceptance means seeing your partner for who they are, including their strengths and challenges, and still holding them in positive regard. This means starting a conversation from a place where you recognize your partner is a good and caring person. It means separating your partner's worth from their challenges, whether you are the one with or without ADHD. It also means both of you are allowed to be yourselves, even though you function differently. This often ties into setting boundaries based on your values and needs, which we'll discuss later in the book.

Think of the Five Relationship Pillars as nutrients that a neurodiverse relationship needs to thrive. This creates an environment where the ADHD partner feels safe and free to express themselves, and the non-ADHD partner feels a sense of partnership. Throughout the upcoming chapters, you will discover how these pillars can help reduce relationship challenges and conflicts.

THE SCIENCE OF NEUROPLASTICITY

All brains have neuroplasticity, which allows the brain to learn and respond to new environments. I like to describe neuroplasticity as various hiking trails in your brain. The skills you already know have created nicely paved roads. We know it's easier to use the well-paved road than to build a new trail that may require clearing and building a path. Our brains tend to take the easiest path when stressed because it is the most accessible, which doesn't necessarily mean you will get to your desired destination more efficiently.

It's important to remember that learning new skills can be uncomfortable at times. Both brains will be asked to learn new methods and communication tools, while discarding the old ones. This can be a challenging and anxiety-producing process. If you are the non-ADHD partner, you may not want to praise your partner for doing something like putting away their shoes, but it will move your relationship in the right direction. Patience and persistence are key. If you are the partner with ADHD, you might want to try an executive function strategy to learn how to make putting away your shoes less challenging.

Remember, the more often you and your partner travel down a new "hiking trail," the clearer the path becomes, creating a new neural network in the brain. When stressed, your neural pathways won't be activated, resulting in the same negative patterns you're trying to avoid. It takes time and practice, but it will be worth it as you move closer to your goals.

- Common issues with neurodiverse couples arise from brain differences and the lack of a common language that works for both brains.

- Understanding how both brains work is helpful in realizing that standard relationship strategies won't work for a neurodiverse couple.

- ADHD brains have weaker executive function skills and tend to lack strategies that will work for their brains, creating stress in a relationship.

- Both partners need to learn and practice new techniques and skills to rewire their relationship.

- The Five Relationship Pillars are essential for creating an environment where the ADHD brain can thrive. They are praise, acknowledgment, games, growth mindset, and positive acceptance.

CHAPTER TWO

In Their Shoes

A neurodiverse couple may experience the same event differently. As you've learned, ADHD brains work harder to complete simple, mundane tasks whereas a neurotypical brain can accomplish the same task without much difficulty. Someone with an ADHD brain might expect a big reward and recognition for completing a chore that their partner considers basic and unworthy of acknowledgment. These unique experiences shape the stories you each tell yourselves about your partner's actions or inactions. This chapter focuses on how each partner feels like they're making sacrifices that often go unnoticed or are deemed insignificant by the other, thereby creating relationship conflict.

"I FEEL MISUNDERSTOOD"

Oftentimes, the partner with ADHD feels unappreciated or unvalued despite how hard they're working to please their partner. When they try to do something nice for their partner, like cook a delicious dinner, instead of appreciation and happiness, their partner gets frustrated and annoyed—often because they've left a mess in the kitchen. Or when they take on more chores thinking it's what their partner wants, they often hear criticism that they didn't finish the job or do it properly. Over time, the ADHD brain loses interest in trying to make their partner happy because it seems like they can never get it right.

Since most people with ADHD don't prioritize the same things as their non-ADHD partner, their efforts in these areas are often to make their partner feel good or satisfied. But instead of receiving recognition and appreciation for their efforts, they are often on the receiving end of their partner's frustration. Many of my clients with ADHD have expressed to me that they are hurt when they believe their partner has misinterpreted their behavior. Here's the perspective of someone with ADHD:

> Clara is not a naturally organized and tidy person, but she kept her home clean and felt comfortable with her style of organization. She knew that when she moved in with Samantha, who prioritized having a clean and tidy home, she would have to adjust to tidying up more often than she was used to. Clara made an effort to keep the common areas neat, but she never felt appreciated for what she was doing. Samantha kept complaining about things being left on the floor or on the dining room table. She never provided positive feedback when the house looked good. When Clara cleaned an area of the house, Samantha would comment on how one part wasn't cleaned well enough. Clara began to feel unappreciated and constantly criticized. She began to wonder why she couldn't have a space to keep things the way she liked. Why was she working so hard to tidy up and clean if she couldn't do it to Samantha's standard? Why couldn't Samantha see the effort she was making?

ADHD Relationships

As discussed in chapter 1, adults with ADHD struggle with the executive function skills that are necessary to maintain a household. Because they haven't been taught effective strategies for their non-neurotypical brain, they are often working harder to complete tasks that are important to their partner. If their partner does not understand how hard they are working, they dismiss their efforts or get frustrated when simple tasks are not completed or performed the way they would like them to be. The relationship pillars of acknowledgment and praise are lacking here.

When the non-ADHD partner isn't acknowledging their effort, the partner with ADHD tends to disconnect and disengage from them. What is the point of trying after so many unsuccessful attempts? This creates a lot of sadness and confusion within the relationship. The non-ADHD partner doesn't understand why simple tasks are hard for their partner, and the partner with ADHD feels defeated because their partner doesn't recognize that they are indeed showing that they love and care for them. Not feeling understood or cared for (even if it's an inaccurate interpretation) will harm the relationship. Because neither partner understands the differences in how their brains function, neither knows to recognize and acknowledge the efforts their partner is making. This leads to the other relationship pillars—praise, games, and growth mindset—being neglected as well.

Remember, the neurological differences in an ADHD brain can make it challenging for them to focus on putting things away. When they are tidying up, they are generally working quite hard. If they only receive criticism in response, a toxic environment is created. Again, a person with ADHD responds best to positive reinforcement, which actually helps them complete difficult tasks. (For more help understanding this, chapter 7 addresses why clutter tends to happen with ADHD.)

STRATEGIES

The following two strategies will help the partner with ADHD share with their partner what they are experiencing within the relationship. Remember, all strategies require practice for new neural pathways to develop. Change won't happen immediately, but with practice these skills will become the new normal.

Fill Your Love Bucket

On a blank piece of paper, spend some time listing things your partner does or could do to make you feel cared for and/or motivated to complete tasks. Also make a list of things your partner may say or do that feels crushing and/or saps your motivation to do something. After you've completed your list, share it with your partner. Request that they try to do more of the things that are helpful for your brain to hear. Here's an example of what this list might look like:

ACTS THAT FILL ME WITH LOVE	ACTS THAT HURT ME
Getting excited about something I did	Focusing on the one thing I didn't do
A big hug	Implying that problems are all my fault
Telling me I am awesome	Saying that I don't care
Saying how much you appreciate me	Saying that I'm lazy
Little surprises or gifts	Complaining about the mess
A thoughtful note	Not acknowledging what I did do that you asked me to do

Smart Relationship Investments

On a blank piece of paper, make a list of the ways you show your partner that you care about them. Think of how challenging each act is for you, rating it from 1 (easy) to 5 (hard). Once you've completed your list, give it to your partner and ask them to rate how much they appreciate each act, with 1 being not much and 5 being a lot.

Before your partner shares their responses with you, ask them to write you a note of appreciation that focuses on how much they appreciate your taking the time and effort to express how you show your love and care. Read this note before looking at their responses.

One of the main goals of any relationship is to be an awesome team, which means learning how each person gives and receives love. Spend a few minutes looking at your partner's rating, and then discuss how each of you can show the other love in a way that will be well received and won't come at a huge emotional cost to either of you. Your efforts may have more impact while being less draining.

The table on the following page is an example of what this might look like after both you and your partner complete the activity.

ACT OF CARE	AMOUNT OF ENERGY IT TAKES (ADHD BRAIN)	HOW MEANINGFUL IT IS TO YOUR PARTNER
Kiss in the morning	1	5
Clean up the kitchen	5	3
Tell you what I appreciate about you	2	5
Do the dishes	3	3
Pay the electric bill	4	4
Plan date nights	2	4
Surprise you with a gift	1	3
Hugs	1	5
Prioritizing tasks that are important to you	4	4

THE NON-ADHD PARTNER
"I FEEL NEGLECTED"

Over time, the non-ADHD partner may begin to feel neglected in the relationship. Feeling solely responsible for maintaining the home can lead to frustration and resentment. They may become annoyed that, although their partner doesn't contribute to their household efforts, they often do tasks for friends or coworkers. The non-ADHD partner can't understand why their partner would be willing and able to complete a task for others but not for them. Eventually, they tend to think their partner doesn't care about them or desire to continue the relationship. Even when they do spend time together, their partner may be so immersed in the millions of things going on around them, including their smartphone, that they aren't focusing on them. Here's a perspective from Samantha's non-ADHD brain:

> Samantha expected there would be a bit more of a mess when Clara moved in. She figured that it would take some time to adjust to each other's habits. She patiently waited

for Clara to pick up her things or complete the household tasks she agreed to do. Instead, she was constantly surprised that items could stay out for weeks. Samantha began to feel alone in the relationship. No matter what she tried, it seemed like she was responsible for chores because Clara wouldn't follow through. When she would let Clara know that she was feeling unsupported, Clara would take on a big project (for example, cleaning inside the kitchen cabinets) that just added more work for Samantha (all the items needed to be put back).

All Samantha wanted was a partner with whom she could share some quality time as well as the burden of household tasks. Even when they would watch a movie together, Clara seemed to be stuck to her phone. Samantha still felt alone even when they were together. She didn't understand why Clara managed to be present for their friends and help them as needed but could not do the same for her. When they had started dating, she felt like the most interesting, most import-ant person in Clara's world, but she didn't feel that was true any longer.

ADHD Relationships

Because the executive functions to initiate and complete tasks are challenging for the ADHD brain, the uninformed partner without ADHD interprets this action as lack of care. They believe that if their partner really was trying, things would get done. They feel hurt that their partner doesn't care how much work they're leaving for them. And when they see their partner doing similar tasks for others, it causes even more pain and strife. It's clear the pillar of acknowledg-ment is missing from the relationship in this scenario.

They may see their partner with ADHD help someone else clean out their garage but not touch the overflowing closet in their own house. This is because the reward system in the ADHD brain requires a bigger reward to become motivated to do a task. Someone with ADHD may be motivated to engage in a challenging task because of a friend's gratitude. Since the ADHD brain may receive criticism instead of praise when doing tasks at home, their brain will not want to engage in tasks that lead to negative consequences.

The lack of praise in the relationship creates a negative environment for the ADHD brain, where it will begin to look for praise in other places instead of from the relationship. As explained in chapter 1, a high reward for an adult with ADHD (a lot of praise) helps their brain do mundane tasks. Without realizing it, the non-ADHD partner may be sending the opposite message because they have not yet learned to express their needs using the Five Relationship Pillars. If they want their partner to be engaged with them, they need to create the right environment.

Weak attention skills also contribute to feelings of neglect. As ADHD brains pay attention to everything, they may seem distracted or unable to relax with their partner. This can be a complete reversal from when the couple first started dating. The ADHD brain loves the novelty and excitement of a new relationship and will be more engaged with their partner when the relationship is fresh. Their hyperfocus may be present during the dating phase, when they are most interested in learning about their partner. Many non-ADHD partners describe this experience as intensely fulfilling and connecting. This is why the relationship pillar of games is necessary in a relationship. Without novel and fun spaces, the ADHD brain can be easily distracted and struggle to connect with their partner.

STRATEGIES

The following two strategies will help the non-ADHD partner explain their experience and needs in a way that won't trigger the "criticism filter" in the ADHD brain.

"I" Statements

Before and after using this strategy, be sure to praise and acknowledge what your partner is doing well. This strategy helps you express what is *not* going well. When sharing with your partner, use "I" statements. An "I" statement consists of three parts:

I feel (state an emotion)
When (state a specific event)
Because (explain why it matters to you)

Remember, everyone is different. An ADHD brain normally doesn't mind mess and clutter, for example, so you will have to explain how it negatively affects you for your partner to care about it. For example, you can say, "I feel frustrated when I have to clean the kitchen alone every night because I need time to wind down from the day."

Watch out for "You" statements when you are making your "I" statements. A "You" statement tells your partner what their intentions or emotions were behind the actions. They tend to sound like, "I feel like you don't care about me because you don't help me clean the kitchen after dinner."

When you want to explain why their actions make you feel neglected, change "You" statements to "The story I am telling myself is . . ." This is a helpful technique to increase connection and understanding while acknowledging that the story you are sharing may or may not be true. This can sound like this: "I am feeling alone in this relationship because when you are checking your phone at dinner, the story I am telling myself is that your phone and social media accounts are more important to you than I am."

▶ TIP Think of what feeling comes up when your partner is late and use it in an "I" statement. For example, "I feel disrespected when you show up late to dinner because I was taught that being on time shows respect."

Get Specific

Think of a few things your ADHD partner could do that would help you feel connected and supported (and help decrease your feelings of neglect). Break each item into three specific behaviors. Remember to make each request using a growth mindset, which establishes that you are in this relationship to grow and learn together. This mindset will help the ADHD brain remember that you are a team. Your suggestions might sound something like this:

NON-SPECIFIC SUGGESTION	SPECIFIC SUGGESTIONS
Help me around the house more.	Put away the laundry after I fold it.
	Dry the dishes after I wash them.
	Vacuum the carpet after I dust.
Show me you care.	Eat dinner without your smartphone present.
	Kiss me good morning.
	Text or call me if you are running late.

▶ **TIP** For a deeper connection, think of fun, novel activities you can do as a couple. Perhaps you can go for a bike ride or hike at an unfamiliar park, or take a cooking or dance class together. It is easier for an ADHD brain to stay engaged and present in different environments.

THE UPSIDE

People with ADHD generally love to make people happy, which is why they often go above and beyond. They are the friend who will find someone else to help you with whatever you need if they aren't available. They are known for making creative gestures and performing acts of love that keep their relationships energized and strong. When a person with ADHD feels valued and appreciated, they put a lot of effort into their relationship.

Your Relationship Goals

It's time to work together to create your relationship goals. You can start this process by identifying what you value as a couple in a relationship. Brainstorm together and keep a list on a piece of paper. Here's a list of values to get you started:

- Adventure
- Authenticity
- Commitment
- Compassion
- Curiosity
- Flexibility
- Growth

- Honesty
- Integrity
- Laughter
- Love
- Loyalty
- Play
- Reliable

- Respect
- Responsibility
- Safety
- Support
- Trust
- Understanding
- Vulnerability

Once you've listed your shared values, think about how you will put these values into practice daily. These will be your relationship goals. Jot them down. Your relationship goals may look something like this:

> We support each other as a team and come from a place where we want both of us to win.
>
> We speak to each other with kindness and respect, and from a place of love.
>
> We do not aim to be perfect, but we aim to be accountable for our actions and make amends as needed.
>
> We seek to understand each other over being "right" because that is how our relationship wins.
>
> We commit to nourishing our relationship daily and making it a priority in our lives.

There are no right or wrong goals. This is about both of you creating your shared vision of what an ideal relationship looks like and being accountable for it.

Your relationship goals will guide your relationship when it comes to talking about the hard stuff. I recommend putting them in a visible place in your home and setting daily reminders on your phone.

The daily reminders will help each of you focus on building the relationship you want—even when it gets tough.

CHAPTER 2 TAKEAWAYS

- Because ADHD and non-ADHD brains are wired differently, they interpret the same event differently, potentially causing pain and disconnection.

- ADHD brains tend to feel misunderstood and rejected when they try to do what their partner wants but feel like it is never good enough.

- Non-ADHD brains tend to incorrectly interpret the lack of executive function skills in ADHD brains as a lack of caring.

- Being specific can help the non-ADHD partner communicate their needs to their partner.

- ADHD brains need positive reinforcement and recognition when they prioritize their partner's needs.

CHAPTER THREE

"I'm Not Enough"

I n this chapter, you will learn how childhood experiences can affect how a person
with ADHD feels about themselves,
along with the strategies they might use
to cope with feelings of inadequacy or
failure. These feelings and coping mechanisms can
create a perfect storm in a relationship when their
neurotypical partner uses certain tactics to try to support them. Understanding how each brain is wired
and using strategies to break cycles can go a long way
in ending toxic relationship dynamics that stem from
these issues.

"I COULD BE BETTER"

Because ADHD brains often struggle with simple tasks, they probably received a lot of negative messages during their formative years. They were likely often told that they were careless, forgetful, lazy, uncaring, unmotivated, or annoying by teachers, parents, and friends. Because of this, many adults with ADHD have internalized a belief that they aren't good enough. They feel inadequate or ashamed because it feels like they can't do things as easily as others. They become hypersensitive to other people's disappointment in them. These experiences can create a criticism filter in their brain (page 8).

Because those with ADHD usually want to avoid disappointing others, many have come up with their own strategies to "be better," such as:

- Setting unrealistic goals of never disappointing others and then emotionally beating themselves up when it happens.
- Using judgment and anger to motivate themselves to do better and avoid disappointing others.
- Worrying about rejection or abandonment if they disappoint their partner, thereby creating the anxiety they need to maintain attention and focus.

These strategies do help an ADHD brain focus on simple tasks because they are using their imagination to turn a small situation into a crisis. Although these strategies may help get the mundane tasks done, they come at a big cost to their self-esteem, mental health, and ultimately to their relationship with others. The following is a perspective from an ADHD brain:

Kristine worried about a lot of things. She worried that she wasn't a good mother. She worried that the house wasn't clean enough. She worried that her husband, Lucas, would be disappointed if she wasn't perfect. She would spend days stressing about something she might forget to avoid "messing up." She put a lot of pressure on herself to be the perfect cook, mom, and homemaker. She spent her days worrying incessantly about how she was failing at everything, hoping it would make her a better person and never disappoint anyone. When her husband made a comment about being out of coffee, it felt like a blow to her whole world. All her failures would be remembered in that moment, and she would add it to her pile of evidence that she wasn't good enough.

ADHD Relationships

The ADHD brain often has intense emotional reactions to their perception of failing or disappointing their partner. Due to their early life experiences with criticism and their desire to avoid disappointing others, they can hear criticism when there isn't any, which can be a confusing experience for the non-ADHD partner.

For instance, let's say that the non-ADHD partner says, "We're out of milk." The ADHD brain may hear that as, "You let us run out of milk." They may then angrily respond that no one told them to pick up milk. This leaves the other person confused. How did their observation that there was no milk create a negative reaction that started an argument? Another possible scenario in reaction to this observation may be the partner with ADHD telling a 15-minute story about why they couldn't get milk like they wanted to. This can also cause confusion for their partner. Why did they feel the need to explain the absence of milk in such detail?

Most adults with ADHD use this defense mechanism to "protect" themselves from disappointing others. They hear blame, criticism, or disappointment from their partner when there may not be any. Because of this pattern in relationships, the non-ADHD partner normally adopts the following two strategies, which don't work long term:

- Avoids saying anything that could potentially hurt their partner's feelings.
- Tries to fix the issue by offering solutions that don't work for an ADHD brain.

To summarize, the pattern looks like this:

1. The ADHD brain hears criticism (that may not be there) and reacts in anger or defensiveness.

2. The non-ADHD brain tries to avoid upsetting their partner by trying ineffective strategies.

3. Repeat until both feel helpless and hurt.

Notice how this pattern completely lacks the Five Relationship Pillars. Praise, acknowledgment, games, growth mindset, and positive acceptance can all help decrease the ADHD brain's criticism filter.

STRATEGIES

These two strategies can help retrain the ADHD brain to embrace failure and recognize when their criticism filter is on. Like learning any skill, these strategies will take practice. Everyone disappoints their partner from time to time, but this doesn't make them any less worthwhile.

"I Failed!"

This strategy is adapted from a warm-up exercise that's often used in improv classes. Each partner takes a bow or curtsey (being as silly or creative as possible with the movement) and states, "I failed." The other person claps loudly and exclaims, "You learned!" Practice this exercise multiple times until it becomes comfortable. The next time either of you feels like a failure, take a bow and say, "I failed." The other person will respond by clapping and saying, "You learned!"

This activity may seem silly, but it is effective at changing patterns and learning to accept failure as an opportunity to grow, instead of adding to the shame you may feel. The moment of silliness helps couples stay connected, reduces defensiveness, and elicits some laughter.

Get the Facts!

If, as the partner with ADHD, you think you hear blame or criticism, ask your partner if you heard them correctly. Repeat back what you heard. Your brain may be drawing from past experiences that make it sound like the statement is bigger than what your partner actually intends. Using the earlier example of being out of milk, your response might sound like: "I want to make sure I am hearing you correctly. Are you saying it is my fault that we do not have any milk? The story I am telling myself is that you are very upset by this."

As the non-ADHD partner, if your partner reacts defensively to something you say, you can help your partner practice this strategy by asking if they heard blame or criticism in your comment.

THE NON-ADHD PARTNER
"I'M BURNED OUT"

Because the neurotypical brain tends to experience situations and events less intensely than an ADHD brain, they may default to the role of supporter. Because work or friendship drama doesn't necessarily impact them as intensely as it does their partner with ADHD, they may not want to burden their partner with "their stuff." Most people don't mind supporting someone they love; it can feel good. However, when the partner with ADHD seems to always be in emotional turmoil, it can begin to wear on their partner. The non-ADHD partner starts feeling frustrated and helpless because their support doesn't seem to make a difference in their loved one's life. If they default to avoiding certain behaviors or not sharing their experiences, the overall well-being of the relationship is affected. This contributes to the supporter burnout that many non-ADHD partners experience. The following is the perspective of a non-ADHD brain:

Lucas tried to be a supportive spouse. He hoped that Kristine's decision to stay at home with the kids would reduce her stress level. He tried to say supportive things when Kristine would become upset or angry over the small stuff. He didn't understand why everything seemed to turn into an argument. He would try to come up with solutions like getting a housekeeper, her going back to work if she wanted, or hiring a nanny. Each one seemed to be hurtful to Kristine and was rejected. Ultimately, Lucas tried to stop saying things that would cause her to get upset.

Lucas began to feel trapped because he couldn't share his experience (like being frustrated with the house being messy) or his wife would be upset for days. He also felt helpless because no matter what he said or did, nothing seemed to work. It seemed like Kristine would move from one crisis to another. He felt like he had no space to ask for support or change because she always was going through something. He wondered if there would ever be a time when Kristine wasn't stressed.

ADHD Relationships

Most adults with ADHD today didn't receive therapy to learn effective strategies for their weaker executive function skills during their formative years. Left to its own devices, the ADHD brain realized that it does better in a crisis and, as a result, developed certain strategies:

Turn mundane tasks into large projects and emergencies to help them focus. For example, waiting until they have no clean clothes before doing laundry; waiting until there are no clean dishes left before washing them; thinking of a future crisis ("If I don't wash this dish, I will get a cockroach infestation"); waiting until a deadline is looming to start a project; or redoing an entire room rather than making a small change.

Imagine rejection or criticism. For example, imagining a loved one would be disappointed or angry if they didn't do a task; believing that if they mess up, their partner will be devastated and leave them. This "motivates" them to avoid the perceived consequence of abandonment.

These strategies may help an adult with ADHD succeed at work, but they will negatively affect their relationship. It can appear to others that ADHD brains are always dealing with something big, so they are in constant need of support and attention. Because ADHD brains use stress to focus, they may not be aware of the effect on others. If someone with ADHD freaks out each morning over finding their keys, it can be draining on their partner's emotional well-being. If the non-ADHD partner doesn't share their life stressors because their partner is already stressed, they will eventually feel like there's no space for them in the relationship.

STRATEGIES

Adults with ADHD function better with routines and schedules (even though they resist them in the beginning). Routine check-ins give each partner an opportunity to share the highs and lows of their day, as discussed in the first strategy. The second strategy is an excellent tool for ascertaining how much support the partner with ADHD needs.

Routine Check-ins

Set aside 5 to 10 minutes each evening for a quick daily check-in as a couple. Try to do it at the same time and in the same environment—for example, when you walk the dog, in bed before you settle in for sleep, or at dinner.

During this check-in, each partner should share something they are grateful for, something they are excited about, and something that was challenging for them. The other partner listens with their full attention. Many people know this type of check-in as "Rose, Bud, Thorn."

Share the Facts

If, as the non-ADHD partner, you are sacrificing something to support your partner, let them know. You may think that your partner needs your support because they are stressed out, but you may be mistaken. This may be normal for them. Asking them if they need your support and then sharing the emotional cost of giving that support can help you both understand what each of you needs in that situation. Here's an example:

"The story I am telling myself is that you need help looking for your keys because you look stressed. I could help you if you really need it, but I am feeling rushed and may be late to work if I help you. Could you let me know how much this would help you?"

THE UPSIDE

Creating a safe environment by using the Five Relationship Pillars helps your partner with ADHD heal from past hurts, forming a deep bond and trust in your relationship. A positive, accepting relationship for someone with ADHD helps unleash the incredible strengths that an ADHD brain has. These benefits come in the form of frequent expressions of intense joy, excitement, and love that the partner with ADHD feels. Adults with ADHD like to do small and big acts of love to make their partner happy. They are amazing at making their partner feel loved, cared for, prioritized, and happy, because they do want to be the best for the one they love.

You Matter Ball Toss

Purchase a new soccer ball and a permanent marker. On the ball, write words representing your relationship goals from chapter 2. Here are some words to get you started:

- Accountable
- Caring
- Considerate
- Fun

- Honest
- Humor
- Love
- Respect

- Responsible
- Supportive
- Teamwork
- Vulnerable

Go outside to toss the ball back and forth. When you catch the ball, look at the word closest to your thumb and share with your partner what you did for them that week that expresses that value, or something they did that you appreciate with respect to that value. For example, if your thumb lands on the word "Respect," you might say that you used your new communication skills when you were frustrated instead of yelling that the dishes were not done. If your thumb lands on the word "Caring," you might say that you picked up your partner's favorite food on Monday to show them how much you care. Or if your thumb lands on "Teamwork," you might tell your partner how much you appreciated their help that morning making the bed.

Do this weekly to gain insight into how each of you thinks of and supports the other. Tossing a ball outdoors can keep you both engaged in this relationship-building activity. To keep things novel and fun, get creative. Perhaps you can high-five or even kiss after each partner shares. Try throwing the ball different ways. You can also time yourself to see how many statements you can get in 10 minutes and see if you can beat your record next time.

- Negative feedback in childhood can make the ADHD brain feel inadequate, leading to a "criticism filter" (hearing criticism where none was intended).

- Many adults with ADHD use stress and anxiety to help them accomplish tasks and sometimes don't actually need their partner's assistance.

- Taking on the role of supporter can lead the non-ADHD partner to a state of burnout, so they need to ask if their support is necessary and, if so, share what the cost would be to them to provide that assistance.

- Routine check-ins to talk about the roses, buds, and thorns of the day can help a neurodiverse couple learn how to effectively support each other.

CHAPTER FOUR

So Distracted

D istraction is what ADHD is known for, and being distracted is what impacts so many areas of a relationship. As discussed in chapter 2, distraction can suggest to a partner that the other person doesn't care about them. It can make transitioning from one activity to another or completing tasks extremely difficult. One of the biggest things that can impact a relationship is being late, which is usually a common occurrence for someone with ADHD. This chapter provides insights into each partner's experience and the impact it can have on the relationship.

Time management becomes even more important in a relationship as responsibilities grow—taking care of a home, planning vacations, caring for children— and therefore increases the likelihood of conflict between partners.

"WHAT WAS I SUPPOSED TO DO?"

The ADHD brain is not very good at judging how long it will take to complete a task. They may pile on activities to make the tasks ahead feel more like a big, exciting puzzle or project. They've likely noticed over the years that if they have downtime during a transition, they'll become distracted and won't get to their next task. A common strategy they come up with is cramming too many things into the day. Here's a typical story from a client with ADHD about their day:

> I had it all figured out. I got the kids to school on time so I went for a coffee, and the line was so long that I was late for work. But I managed to call in for my meeting while driving, and I don't think anyone noticed. Then a friend wanted to go to lunch, so I decided that I would work during my kid's basketball game that night to make up for the time. I hadn't seen my friend in a while and normally they are busy so I couldn't really say no. Unfortunately, at the school during the game, I couldn't get a Wi-Fi signal, and it was so noisy I couldn't concentrate. My kid wouldn't let me work and other parents kept interrupting me. I needed to finish this project, and I am so stressed out that I couldn't get it done. To top it off, I yelled at my kids because I couldn't work and felt bad about it. No matter how hard I try, I keep failing.

Fitting several mundane tasks into a day is like working on an exciting and novel puzzle, which helps the ADHD brain focus. The "win" of figuring out how to accomplish a lot of tasks provides the dopamine boost the ADHD brain needs to stay motivated (page 51). This is why some people with ADHD are known for being really active, busy, and able to accomplish a lot. The downside of this strategy is not accounting for transition time, unexpected events, and how much time is actually in a day. Cramming too many tasks and events into the day can have big consequences and result in upset or even disaster.

If someone with ADHD doesn't use their misguided strategy of overscheduling their day, they tend to look at something on their to-do list, not start it, and become distracted by something else. Let's say they need to start dinner but notice the full laundry basket in the hall leading to the kitchen; they carry it to the bedroom to start putting the laundry away, but there's a photo album on the bed. They start flipping through the album, when they hear a notification sound on their phone and go in search of their phone.

ADHD Relationships

The experience of continuous distractions can frustrate both partners. The neurotypical partner starts to believe they can't count on their partner for simple tasks because they aren't getting them done. The neurotypical brain sees a simple solution: "Stop trying to do everything at once; be more realistic with tasks so you won't be frustrated." However, that solution doesn't work for the ADHD brain. Having a big reward by accomplishing a lot decreases their default mode network (page 5), which makes it easier for them to succeed at mundane tasks. If they slow down, it's the perfect opportunity to get distracted.

Unlike the ADHD brain, the neurotypical brain can filter out unnecessary stimuli to focus on a small task and get a dopamine reward when it is completed. The executive function skill of organization and planning is required to effectively organize one's day, coupled with the executive function of self-control to ignore more interesting activities. Without these strong executive functions, other supportive systems, like those discussed in the upcoming strategies, are needed to reduce distraction. Although cramming everything into the day might sometimes be effective, it often comes at a cost.

STRATEGIES

Most environments are set up for the success of the neurotypical brain, so when I work with people who have ADHD my key phrase is "Make the environment work for you." Creating an environment in which the ADHD brain can thrive is life changing for the person and the couple. An ADHD coaching group or a therapist can be extraordinarily helpful here. In the meantime, here are two strategies to get started.

Make a Schedule

A schedule can support someone with weak organization and planning skills. The more routine you can make a task, the more it becomes like second nature, and the easier it is for you to accomplish your to-dos.

Use a smartphone app, a calendar, or physical planner to create a schedule that works for you. (The Resources section on page 132 includes recommendations that work well for an ADHD brain.) Keep your schedule simple. You may want to pile everything on, but try to stick to just the basics. When you see your schedule laid out, you may realize that it's nearly impossible to do everything you want to do in one day. This can help you omit a few things that aren't as essential. Having a schedule can also help you transition from one activity to another because it's a visual reminder of what's up next.

What's interesting is that the ADHD brain thrives with a schedule but often resists following one. So, if you don't like the idea of having a daily schedule, choose just one day a week to follow a schedule. Plan a reward for completing all your to-dos that day. After a few weeks, look back and consider the difference between your scheduled and unscheduled days.

Fun Downtime

Choose an activity you enjoy that is relatively easy to start and stop and one that can be performed virtually anywhere. When you have downtime between tasks, turn to this activity to avoid being distracted by other things. Here are a few ideas:

• Scroll through social media like Facebook or TikTok.
• Read a few pages of a book.
• Listen to music.
• Text a friend.
• Play a game on your phone or in a puzzle book.
• Stretch or move (e.g., jumping jacks or walk).

▶ **TIP** Your brain will lose track of time, so you need to set it up for success. If you don't have a natural reminder to transition to the next activity, such as someone calling you in for your appointment, use a timer. An auditory or visual reminder will bring your attention back to where it needs to be.

THE NON-ADHD PARTNER
MANAGING TIME

When their partner is consistently arriving late at events or takes a long time to complete a task, the neurotypical partner can start feeling helpless and hurt. Some cultures show their care and respect by showing up on time, so lateness can also be embarrassing when family is involved. Most non-ADHD partners start telling themselves that their partner just doesn't care about them, their family and friends, or the activity planned.

When a couple is planning a wedding, this experience can be intensified. There are many important events to show up to that represent a couple's love and commitment. In other cases, if the couple has children, the conflict can become magnified if the ADHD partner's lateness somehow impacts their children. Let's take a look from a non-ADHD perspective:

During her engagement to Oscar, Natasha grew distraught, confused, and hurt. She had been so excited to marry him, but planning the wedding put a dark cloud over their relationship. They were always fighting. She pleaded with him to show up to events on time, whether it was cake tasting or to the engagement party her parents had planned. She explained that others commented on how often he was late, and she was embarrassed. Natasha told Oscar that showing up late symbolized to her that he didn't care about the wedding or joining her family. Oscar promised to be on time for the next big event but failed to do so.

Instead of looking forward to her wedding day, Natasha was dreading it. She imagined everyone looking at their watches while they waited for him to show up. Looking further into the future, she wondered if Oscar would be there for their future children's many milestones. How could it be so hard for him to get where he needed to be and when?

ADHD Relationships

Weak organization and planning, attention, and self-control can all impact the ADHD brain when it comes to managing time effectively. The other executive function needed to manage time is working memory. Due to the lack of fully developed working memory, someone with ADHD tends to remember just the major task that needs to be done and forgets the little steps in between. This often means they misjudge how long a task will take, believing it will take less time than it actually requires—despite how many times they have experienced the consequences of this misjudgment. Here's an example:

Natasha wanted to help Oscar be on time. She decided to provide multiple warnings of a time countdown before they needed to leave for an event. One time, her fiancé acknowledged the time warning while he was watching TV and even said he was ready to go. When it was time to go, Natasha watched Oscar go upstairs to start showering and shaving! How was this even possible? Determined, she switched her strategy. She stopped asking if he was ready. Instead, she would ask him if he had completed each task he needed to do in order to be ready: Did he shower? Did he brush his teeth? Did he shave? With each of those tasks, she would set time reminders. She was thrilled when this method actually worked.

Neurotypical brains know the steps they need to take to get ready for an event, making it seem "obvious" or "common sense." But someone with a weak working memory may forget these steps when calculating how much time they need. When Oscar was watching TV and telling Natasha he was ready, he really believed he was ready. He thought it would take him only a minute to change and put on shoes. But when he got up to the master closet, he saw the shower and realized he needed to bathe. Then he looked in the mirror and realized he needed to shave. In Oscar's mind, it didn't take long for him to get ready. His weak working memory led to his forgetting to factor in all the things he would need to do to "be ready" to go out. This is what caused him to be late—all the time.

STRATEGIES

The first strategy supports the partner with ADHD by providing concrete steps they can follow to get out of the door on time. The second strategy calls in the relationship pillar of positive acceptance by realizing that each partner is a unique individual who views and manages time differently than the other.

Lists and Timers

Managing time and planning out the day can be very challenging for someone with ADHD. Work together to create a checklist and reminders for tasks the ADHD partner tends to underestimate how long it will take to complete. This list should be accessible to the ADHD partner at all times.

As you create the checklist as a team, remember to maintain a growth mindset. The idea is to work together in a way that will help you both learn and grow. With the pillars of praise and acknowledgment at the forefront, you will recognize your combined effort to support each other. However, if your partner doesn't want your support in this area after discussing it, it's important to respect their decision—that's positive acceptance.

There are many great apps geared for children, such as Brili, that can also help the adult with ADHD create a morning schedule. They can plan their routine in the app using parent mode and then follow along in kid mode, which can help their ADHD brain maintain focus. It also has a built-in timer for refocusing on the task at hand, just in case the ADHD brain gets distracted. The app also shows you how many more things are left to do, which supports a weak working memory. Hopefully, as awareness around adult ADHD increases, apps like this will be geared specifically for adults, but in the meantime, these kid-friendly apps can be helpful.

▶ **TIP To avoid being your ADHD partner's verbal reminder, make sure the steps of each task are clearly spelled out on their checklist.**

Independence

Waiting on your partner with ADHD to get ready so that you can leave the house often leads to feelings of helplessness and frustration. Accept that leaving on time may always be a challenging task for your partner and come up with a backup plan to help you take care of yourself. Here is one way to phrase your plan:

- "This is an event that I cannot be late for." (For example, a surprise birthday party, a meeting, or a concert.)
- "I will give you a 10-minute warning that it's time to leave and then a 1-minute warning that it's time to leave. When that minute is up, I will leave—with or without you."
- "I will say 'I love you' before I leave without any anger or resentment. I will recognize that running late does not reflect how you feel about us."

Discuss this backup plan with your partner in advance. Let them share with you what they think the best way to phrase each statement would be so that they can hear it well. Positive acceptance from both partners helps you honor and respect that you each do things differently.

It may be difficult, but you need to follow through on this. Being consistent makes it easier to do over time and provides positive reinforcement for your partner to get ready on time because, if they do, they get to leave with you!

▶ **TIP** If being on time is your priority (not your partner's), express your appreciation of their efforts in trying to accommodate your needs. This nurtures the relationship pillars of praise and acknowledgment.

THE UPSIDE
Knowing how to work well as a neurodiverse couple can lead to amazing accomplishments. The ADHD brain can hyperfocus when something interests them, allowing them to accomplish big tasks and challenging projects. What's more, ADHD brains thrive in emergencies and crises. They are able to navigate challenging situations with relative ease, keeping everyone safe.

A Shared Calendar

Download a shared calendar app on each of your devices or use a paper calendar. Use this calendar to schedule events and set up reminders as a couple. This is an easy and effective way to be visually reminded of upcoming plans that affect you both.

It's not going to help if the partner with ADHD is expected to be on time for everything on your calendar because that won't be effective or acknowledge your differences. So, together, pick what's important for you as a couple to be on time for—for example, a meeting with your child's teacher, a dinner party at a friend's house, an appointment at the DMV, etc. Remember, being on time requires extra effort from the ADHD partner, so they will need to use strategies that work for their brain.

Celebrate the success! If you get out the door on time as a couple, the neurotypical partner needs to provide the ADHD brain with praise and positive reinforcement. This honors the relationship pillars of praise and acknowledgment by providing positive feedback for their effort. It also helps motivate the ADHD brain to try again next time.

▶ **TIP** Don't fall into the trap of turning everything into a couple issue. The partner with ADHD needs to be responsible for their own time management when it isn't a couple issue. The non-ADHD partner doesn't need to be responsible for getting their partner to work, for instance, and they aren't responsible for protecting the ADHD partner from getting into a bad mood as a result of their being late.

CHAPTER 4 TAKEAWAYS

- Weak executive function skills make it challenging for the ADHD brain to transition from one task to another without becoming distracted.

- The ADHD brain generally doesn't recognize how long a task will take. Using schedules, lists, and reminders can help a person with ADHD plan and succeed.

- To protect the relationship from conflicts around time management, it's a good idea for the neurotypical partner to establish a plan to leave on time for something—with or without their partner.

- An ADHD coaching group or a therapist can help you create an environment in which the ADHD brain can thrive.

CHAPTER FIVE

The Emotional Roller Coaster

E motional outbursts have the potential to do the quickest and most damage to your relationship. Without knowing how to communicate in a healthy and productive way, intense negative emotions can lead to ugly verbal attacks between loved ones. Depending on how each partner fights, it can get ugly and painful fast. I refer to this as emotionally beating someone up. Every couple needs to learn how to manage emotional conflict well, of course, but this is especially true for neurodiverse couples. People with ADHD often experience intense emotions. This chapter explains why and also provides tools to help regulate emotions without damaging your relationship.

THE ADHD PARTNER
"I CAN'T CONTROL MY EMOTIONS"

Generally, emotions are felt more intensely by someone with ADHD. They may experience extreme joy and excitement followed by extreme disappointment or anger. It can be a roller-coaster ride for them and others around them. Many adults with ADHD have learned to hide their intense negative feelings from others, like friends and coworkers.

When a couple begins living together, it may be harder to hide the intense negative emotions that lead to outbursts, yelling, or straight-out being mean. Normally, the partner with ADHD tries hard to prevent the outbursts at home, but with ineffective strategies they will eventually come out. Adults with ADHD normally feel guilty about their behavior once they've calmed down and may be able to apologize (be accountable) or may blame the other person for their outburst (be defensive and dismissive). How they express themselves depends on how much they've learned with regard to emotional recognition and regulation. Let's consider this ADHD perspective:

Michael was waiting for Luke to come over. He was super excited to go out and celebrate the end of the workweek. When Luke texted to say he was leaving in 30 minutes, Michael felt an intense reaction of anger, resentment, and disappointment. Luke would arrive an hour later than Michael had expected. Even though they hadn't confirmed a time to meet, Michael started to think of all the things Luke did wrong and how he constantly disappointed him. Luke obviously didn't care about him or he would have already been here, or at least expressed disappointment that he was at work instead of with him. Blinking away tears, Michael tried to distract himself but it didn't really work. When Luke finally arrived, Michael began to yell at him, telling him how horrible he was and how no one thought he was good enough to be his boyfriend. Michael was so angry. He dismissed any explanation from Luke, and just wanted him to feel as bad as he did.

ADHD Relationships

Intense emotional reactions are part of all intimate relationships, both the good (big romantic gestures) and the bad (angry verbal attacks). However, with their weaker executive function skills like emotional regulation, working memory, and attention, adults with ADHD can experience more emotional outbursts than their neurotypical partner.

Someone with ADHD may have emotional outbursts when they feel disappointed or unnoticed—for example, if they're looking forward to seeing their partner and plans are canceled or if they don't receive recognition when they're making an effort to please their partner. Because they often go above and beyond to please their partner and try to avoid disappointing them, a person with ADHD will try to keep their challenging or negative feelings about the relationship to themselves. Eventually, however, those negative feelings come out—usually in an emotional outburst that seems, to the other partner, to come from nowhere.

This emotional roller coaster can make it hard for the neurotypical partner to be supportive. When the ADHD "brakes" don't work, it can leave the non-ADHD partner feeling helpless and confused. They will struggle with how to provide feedback to avoid blow-out fights or intense responses. Over time, negative outbursts weigh heavily on a relationship, and even moments of joy and connection can't overcome hurtful words said in anger.

A pattern of angry outbursts is much less likely to occur if the partner with ADHD feels secure in the relationship—especially when the Five Relationship Pillars are present. When the pillars of positive acceptance and growth mindset are strong, it is easier for both partners to share their feelings. If the pillars of praise and acknowledgment are strong, the partner with ADHD gets the positive feedback and praise they need when they share their concerns or disappointments. This positive reaction motivates them to continue having honest conversations. When the relationship pillar of games is present, the couple has quality time to connect and see that their relationship can thrive after conflict.

STRATEGIES

Emotional regulation is a skill that can be learned and developed over time. Although the partner with ADHD may struggle more in this area, both partners can benefit from the following strategies. There are many great resources on how to develop or strengthen emotional regulation. Like any other skill, you need to practice it often to remember how to use it properly when intense emotions arise.

Calm Down Space

A "calm down space" is an area in your home stocked with items and activities that will help you regulate your emotions. Regulation doesn't mean the emotion goes away. It means you are able to feel the emotion and decrease its intensity to better understand what you need and then make behavioral choices that align with your relationship goals.

In this space, you may find it helpful to hang a poster that depicts different emotions to help you identify how you are feeling. You can keep a notebook or journal nearby to write down what you are feeling in the form of an "I" statement (page 30).

Having sensory objects and visual reminders in the area can help you regulate how you are feeling. Here are a few ideas:

> **Glitter bottles.** Shake the bottle and watch the glitter settle while you take deep breaths.

> **Clay.** Sculpt your feelings. If your feeling was a sculpture, what would it look like? Bring awareness to how the clay feels in your hands.

> **Mindfulness exercise.** Download an app such as Headspace to walk you through a mindfulness exercise.

> **Bubbles.** Blow bubbles. Imagine each emotion on the surface of the bubble and pop them one by one.

Scented lotion. Rub scented lotion on your hands and, holding your hands near your nose, take three deep breaths. Notice how you feel afterward.

You will learn over time what helps you calm your intense emotions. Perhaps music and a scented candle or essential oil diffuser will work best for you. Or maybe breathing and mindfulness activities will be your go-to.

▶ **TIP** You don't have to wait for intense emotions to occur before using the space. You can go there daily to check in with any emotion you are experiencing and use your tools as needed.

Deflate Your Emotional Balloon

Purchase a bag of balloons. When you're feeling intense emotions, go someplace where you can be alone and take out one of the balloons. As you blow into it, assign something you are upset about to each breath. See how big the balloon gets.

Now deflate it, little by little, stating how you feel about each thing that happened, using "I" statements (page 30). The goal is to not let the balloon get so big that it explodes. The best way to do that is by letting things out slowly, one at a time.

If your partner is available, you can bring the filled balloon to your partner, who, having read this strategy, will understand its purpose. As you make your "I" statements and deflate the balloon, keep in mind your relationship goals (page 33) and the Five Relationship Pillars to help you frame your feelings and experiences in a way that aligns with your relationship goals.

▶ **TIP** When you're in the moment and notice that something bothers you but decide not to share it with your partner at that time, imagine yourself blowing into your balloon and then deflating it. Later, when you're feeling calm, share with your partner what you were experiencing.

"WE FIGHT OFTEN"

In the early stages of a neurodiverse relationship, the non-ADHD partner may enjoy the thrill of their partner's energy and intense expressions of love, interest, and care. However, once they start living together, the stress and negativity their partner brings to the home may come as a surprise. Wanting to be helpful, the neurotypical partner may try to offer solutions or encourage their partner to see the bright side of things. It doesn't make sense to them that a small change in plans (like not having their favorite meal at a restaurant) could ruin a romantic evening. The non-ADHD brain has the working memory needed to see the bigger picture and can't understand why their partner can't do the same. Over time, many non-ADHD partners feel defeated and exhausted by the negative cycle that seems to bring everyone down. Here's how this looks from a non-ADHD perspective:

Luke felt helpless and confused. He loved Michael but didn't understand what set him off. He felt wounded by Michael's words whenever he tore into him. Luke tried to avoid the behaviors he thought were the problem, but Michael's intense emotional outbursts continued. Sometimes, Luke was able to answer a phone call from a friend without an emotional reaction from Michael. Other times, if he answered a call, Michael would be upset at him. Because of this, Luke privately decided to not answer phone calls from friends when he was with Michael. As time passed, he felt resentful that he had changed his behavior and spoke to his friends less often. When he expressed this to Michael, Michael became defensive and explained it wasn't about the phone call and gave such a long explanation that Luke couldn't follow. Luke was a linear, concrete thinker and couldn't understand how answering the phone wasn't the issue, despite Michael's explanations. Privately, he thought it was just easier to not answer the phone to avoid a conflict because he couldn't understand how to determine when it would or wouldn't be okay.

ADHD Relationships

It's difficult to break a negative cycle in a relationship once it has begun. Many non-ADHD partners complain of feeling worn out by the constant fighting that tends to occur when the Five Relationship Pillars are not present. They may feel as if anything they say or do just turns into a fight. Even doing something their partner requested, such as going to the movies, can turn into a fight if their partner detects any negativity in their tone. Even if the partner with ADHD is amazing in many ways, their negativity can lead to hurt feelings and resentment. Feeling emotionally beat up can bring anyone to a breaking point. At this stage, the non-ADHD partner will likely emotionally "hit back" when they feel attacked, which leads to intense, cruel fights.

I've worked with many couples who have reached this breaking point mostly because they weren't aware of how important it is to maintain the Five Relationship Pillars in their neurodiverse partnership. Even knowing the pillars, it is a challenge to maintain the relationship pillar of positive acceptance when the neurotypical partner is feeling emotionally beat up. When each person takes emotional punches, it can make the emotional storm worse for the ADHD brain. This tends to increase their criticism filter, which leads to even more frequent fights.

Self-control is necessary to delay an impulsive emotional reaction, which can provide immediate relief but also long-term damage. Self-control helps regulate the emotion and choose a behavior that supports the long-term goals of the relationship. Therefore, a person with ADHD may recognize their angry outbursts are hurting their partner and want to stop the emotional roller coaster, but they are unable to execute their promise. If the non-ADHD partner can reflect when the ADHD "brakes" aren't working, sometimes it can help their partner use their tools, like their calm down space, before responding.

STRATEGIES

It's important for those on the receiving end of frequent emotional outbursts to make sure that they are taking care of themselves. It can be tough for anyone to weather repeated negative emotional outbursts from their partner, and they shouldn't have to. The following strategies may be challenging the first few times, but with continued use, negative cycles can be broken.

Boundaries

Establish a few boundaries. Think about what behaviors you will not tolerate from your partner to protect the relationship and uphold the relationship pillar of positive acceptance. Write these behaviors down to solidify them in your mind. Now, think about what will happen if your partner crosses that boundary. Write that down as well. When you are satisfied that you've addressed what's most important to you, discuss this with your partner. (Wait until things are good, not when you both are already stressed.) Here is an example of how this might sound:

"If I am called names or hear hurtful things about my character, or if I am being spoken to in a way that feels disrespectful to me or goes against our relationship goals, I will not engage in further conversation. I will leave the room/space by telling you that I love you and reminding you that I will listen when we are both in a good space to talk. I will do this to protect our relationship. I know you do not want to hurt me but sometimes your 'brakes' fail you. I need a way to protect myself so we can continue to have the relationship we both want."

▶ **TIP** Ask your partner how they might best receive feedback from you if they cross one of your boundaries. For example, they may want a reminder that their "brakes" are failing them before you leave the room.

Co-Regulation

👍 ⊕

You can help regulate your partner's intense emotion by leaning into the emotion and naming or reflecting back your partner's emotion and intensity. It may seem counterintuitive to put more focus on it, but it can be helpful. Here's how this might sound:

"I see that you are very disappointed that I was later than expected getting here tonight. I know you hoped I would be over earlier. You missed me and wanted to spend time with me. Of course you are upset and disappointed." Then you can offer a hug, a kiss, or something that your partner finds calming. Remind yourself that they may need more time than you would to regulate their emotions.

Notice that you are not minimizing the emotion, which would only exacerbate the situation because your partner would now feel misunderstood, as well. Minimization sounds like this: "We never settled on a time to meet! You're overreacting. I'm here, aren't I?"

Also, try to avoid negative feedback. You may need to use your own emotional regulation skills and self-control to do this. Negative feedback sounds like: "Why do you have to ruin everything? It's Friday night and we have the entire weekend together!"

After you've leaned into the emotion, continue to focus on the relationship pillar of positive acceptance. You might say something along these lines: "I love how much you want to see me and spend time together. I know you may need some time to be upset and disappointed about what time I was able to leave work. Let me know if there is anything I can do to support you."

THE UPSIDE

Knowing how to support each other emotionally fosters safety and intimacy in your relationship. The plus side of an intense "feeler" is the unbridled joy, excitement, and love they bring to a relationship. These are qualities other couples have to work hard to sustain, but it often comes easily to someone with ADHD when they feel secure in their relationship.

Taking Out the Trash

Making amends after a fight is more important than preventing one. Learning how to repair the hurt is a critical skill in any type of relationship. For this exercise, set up three buckets with the following labels:

- Outside our control (person, environment, etc.)
- Accountability for (insert one partner's name)
- Accountability for (insert the other partner's name)

Cut a few pieces of paper into strips, and on a full-size sheet, write "Relationship Wins" at the top.

Name aloud the current situation you both wish to make amends for. Now, on a strip of paper, write down a feeling you are having about the current issue. Use as many strips of paper as you each need.

Next, take turns stating what you've written on the strips of paper, crumpling it up, and tossing it into the appropriate bin. Each time one of you uses an "I" statement or communicates within the guidelines of your relationship goals, give yourself a point on the "relationship win" sheet. Score another point each time one of you takes accountability for something. Being accountable is important in managing conflict in any relationship. It can be helpful to see how many strips of paper go into the "outside our control" bucket. We often blame difficult situations on our partner that are really out of their control.

Obviously, the goal of this exercise is to rack up points. Keep it interesting to engage the ADHD brain. You can try tossing the paper from farther distances or backward over your shoulder. If you use trash bins and large pieces of paper, you can even use a tennis racket. If it's a good shot, celebrate with high fives, kisses, or silly dances.

Here's how this exercise would look for Luke and Michael after a fight over a phone call:

LUKE: *A friend called me.* ("Outside Our Control")

LUKE: *I did not check with you if it impacted our plans if I took the call.* ("Accountability for Luke" and "Relationship Win" point)

MICHAEL: *I did not use an "I" statement on how it made me feel that you answered the phone. I was feeling uncared for because I was planning on telling you something important.* ("Accountability for Michael" and "Relationship Win" point)

MICHAEL: *I recognize I unfairly blamed you for not reading my mind. My ADHD "brakes" failed!* ("Outside Our Control," "Accountability for Michael," and "Relationship Win" point)

CHAPTER 5 TAKEAWAYS

- It's often challenging for someone with ADHD to regulate their emotions because their "brakes" (executive function skills) aren't working well enough to slow down the emotional reaction.

- Practicing calming strategies decreases emotional outbursts and intense fights, and increases closeness and stability.

- Communicating your boundaries to your partner and following through on consequences for not upholding them protects you and your relationship from further harm.

- To avoid a negative spiral that turns into constant fighting and putdowns, both partners need to regulate their emotions and interact with each other from the foundation of the Five Relationship Pillars.

CHAPTER SIX

Out of Sight, Out of Mind

When a neurodiverse couple needs to work together as a team to manage life's responsibilities, the ADHD partner's tendency to be forgetful can become a major pain point in their relationship. The non-ADHD partner generally feels the brunt of incomplete tasks, leading to a lot of frustration. The inability to work as a team to manage household and life responsibilities can lead the neurotypical partner to feel quite alone in the relationship. This chapter explains why the ADHD brain tends to be forgetful and how to work together to overcome the challenges presented by this weak executive function.

THE ADHD PARTNER
"I CAN'T REMEMBER"

One of the most challenging and frustrating experiences for someone with ADHD is dealing with the combination of having weak
attention and working memory. Not being able to focus on one thing
(attention) means they miss pertinent information when they get distracted. Not being able to remember things (working memory) means
that if they did manage to pay attention, they may quickly forget it.

In school, someone with ADHD may have needed to reread the
same page in a book dozens of times because their brains couldn't
remember what they had just read. In a relationship, it may look like
they "forget" important information their partner has told them.
In reality, they're not trying to be inconsiderate or not listen; it just
happens. It's a frustrating experience for the partner with ADHD, especially if it impacts those they care about. When they don't remember
something, they may get defensive about their memory when it differs
from their partner's. And, even when they do remember details, like
going to a couple's therapy appointment, their brain is already struggling with time management. Here's a typical ADHD story:

> When LeeAnn and Scott moved in together, Scott was
> pleasantly surprised that LeeAnn would make him lunch to
> take to work every day. Unfortunately, no matter what he did,
> he managed to forget his lunch. He tried a million different
> things to remember and would ask LeeAnn to remind him.
> She grew tired of reminding him. Sometimes Scott would
> remember to bring the lunch but then would forget it in his
> car instead of bringing it into the office. Sometimes he would
> bring it to work and then forget he brought it and eat at the
> cafeteria instead. He could see that his forgetting the lunch
> was upsetting LeeAnn. If only LeeAnn could understand he
> wasn't doing it on purpose. He would normally run back into
> the house several times every morning to grab something
> he had forgotten before he actually left for work. He wished
> LeeAnn could see that forgetting the lunch she had so
> thoughtfully made for him wasn't a reflection on how much
> he appreciated the caring gesture.

ADHD Relationships

A weak working memory can cause a lot of conflict in a relationship because each person's memory is different. Arguments sound like this on repeat:

"I told you that your lunch was in the fridge."

"No, you didn't."

"Yes, I did."

It can be unnerving for the ADHD brain to realize that they actually don't remember. It takes a huge leap of trust to believe their partner's words instead of their own memory. Even if the partner with ADHD knows their memory isn't great, they often feel blamed for forgetting and/or aren't even aware of how many things they've missed.

The neurotypical partner may get their feelings hurt when their partner doesn't remember events that are important to them. They tend to incorrectly interpret forgetfulness as a sign that their partner doesn't believe their relationship is important, without understanding that the ADHD partner's working memory is the issue. Forgetfulness is not an indicator of how much the partner with ADHD loves and cares about them.

Honoring the relationship pillars of acknowledgment and positive acceptance can make for a healthier relationship. To ensure that you're working as a team, both partners need to understand how poor working memory impacts the ADHD brain. And the neurotypical partner needs to look at their partner as a whole, complete, and good person despite their executive function challenges.

If possible, neurodiverse couples should try to find the humor in memory-related situations. I work with a couple whose wife still jokes about how her husband forgot she had a sister for the first two years of dating. She fondly says, "I know his reactions were genuine because it was the exact same response every time I mentioned my sister!" But, on a serious side, not remembering things is tough and sometimes scary. It can be a challenge for adults with ADHD to remember to take their medication every day. The ADHD brain needs compassion and support, even if it can be a frustrating experience for the couple.

STRATEGIES

It is helpful for the partner with ADHD to acknowledge that their difficulty remembering things and how they deal with that impacts both partners' lives. Here are two strategies that can help the partner with ADHD strengthen their working memory to help reduce conflict in the relationship. The first strategy generally helps people with ADHD improve their memory. The second strategy helps them avoid the emotional roller coaster that can accompany a weak memory and lead to conflict.

Pair Your Activities

Most adults with ADHD have had enough reinforcement to remember to do certain things every day, such as brushing their teeth twice a day. So, if you need to remember something, pair it with an activity you already do that you don't have to remember. Here are a few examples of how to pair visual reminders with your everyday activities:

• If you need to remember to take medicine, place the medicine bottle by your toothbrush.
• To remember to take your lunch with you when you leave for work, put your car keys in your lunch bag.
• Put a note on your bathroom mirror about an important task you need to do that day.

Teamwork!

When your partner gets angry with you for forgetting something, you will likely feel blamed or accused of forgetting on purpose, which can lead to an emotional outburst that starts a fight. Instead, explain to your partner that encouraging you and positively supporting you as you navigate this challenge can make all the difference. Your partner's efforts will go a long way in strengthening all Five Relationship Pillars.

Ask your partner to rephrase memory issues as a challenge that you can tackle together instead of immediately getting upset that you forgot again. Let's say you purchased a head of broccoli with the intention of cooking it as a side dish with dinner, but the broccoli was tucked away in the produce drawer, and you forgot about it. The broccoli goes bad. This isn't the first time something like this has happened. Instead of blaming you, your partner can say something along these lines: "Let's work as a team. Neither of us wants food to go to waste. Let's come up with a way that works for both of our brains to avoid that in the future." Then, as a team, you can work together to challenge this issue.

If your partner starts to lay the blame on you for something forgotten, you can playfully say, "I know my memory is way better than yours, so let me remind you that we are working as a team!"

THE NON-ADHD PARTNER
"PLEASE REMEMBER"

As a relationship moves into a domestic partnership, responsibilities and tasks grow exponentially. Add kids to the mix, and the list of to-dos becomes never-ending. Many neurotypical partners start with compassion and understanding when projects or tasks don't get done around the house. They assume it is an occasional occurrence or because their partner is stressed. After all, everyone forgets things now and then. However, things change over time as the non-ADHD partner begins to believe that nothing will ever get done. In the beginning, they often try the following strategies to "fix" the problem, not realizing that they won't work for their ADHD partner's brain:

- Avoid mentioning the task because they don't want to be a nag.
- Avoid talking about their feelings because they fear their ADHD partner's defensive reaction.
- Do the task themselves (referred to as "overfunctioning").

These behaviors can leave the non-ADHD partner feeling burned out and resentful that they are left carrying the burden of all the tasks and details in the household. After all, these items are generally not fun, even if they are easier for a neurotypical brain to do. This experience can create more conflict when the couple has to accomplish an even bigger task, such as refinancing the home or making major home improvements. Let's look at this from a non-ADHD perspective:

> When LeeAnn asked Scott to help with a task, she expected it to be done, especially since she rarely asked for help around the house. Usually, Scott would forget about the task or half-finish it. LeeAnn began to believe she couldn't depend on Scott. When she did ask for Scott's help with something, it just created more work for her; she would eventually have to finish the project herself. It was just easier for her to do it herself. Over time, she began to feel as if Scott just didn't care about her. Each task she did herself reminded her that she had to do it all. Putting away the milk left out on the counter, moving shoes to their place so no one trips over them—it never seemed to end!

ADHD Relationships

The negative cycle of balancing household responsibilities looks like this for a neurodiverse couple:

1. The non-ADHD partner asks the partner with ADHD to handle a task.

2. The non-ADHD partner expresses frustration that the task didn't get done.

3. The partner with ADHD perceives the complaint as criticism and becomes defensive.

4. The non-ADHD partner perceives the defensiveness as dismissive or aggressive.

5. The non-ADHD partner reacts by overfunctioning to avoid a fight and to get the task done but feels unsupported.

6. Repeat until both partners explode over the chores.

Notice how this cycle does not incorporate any of the Five Relationship Pillars. If the pillars were present, this cycle wouldn't get started in the first place. The non-ADHD partner needs to bring up topics that frustrate them, of course, since it is important to share how they are feeling; they simply need to use good communication skills (for example, "I" statements) and let the Five Relationship Pillars drive what they say.

Issues with forgetting can involve a number of things the ADHD brain has trouble with, including working memory, distraction, negative feedback, and organization and planning. This is why conflict around forgetting is so common in neurodiverse couples. A lot of brain differences are working against the couple! It makes it challenging for them to work as an efficient team to do what needs to get done. What seems simple or common sense to a non-ADHD brain is challenging for someone with ADHD. This is why the pillars of acknowledgment and praise are so important here.

STRATEGIES

Oftentimes, a neurotypical partner will make ultimatums or threaten severe consequences if their partner doesn't start remembering to do things. Although this may be effective in the short term to get help around the house, it can have long-term negative consequences because it isn't in alignment with the Five Relationship Pillars. Both partners can work toward changing how they manage tasks and forgetfulness with the following strategies.

Oops, You Forgot Again!

Think back to a time when you were upset that someone forgot something that was important to you, but when they apologized you felt better about the situation. It doesn't help your relationship if your partner becomes defensive and you both spin into a negative cycle of blame and defensiveness, so discuss some ways your partner might acknowledge that they forgot something that will help you accept and move past it. Here are some examples that have been helpful for others:

A statement of recognition and validation. For example, "I am sorry that it didn't get done. My memory makes it hard for both of us. I see that it impacted you by creating more work for you to do. That sucks, and I am sorry."

Humor. Make a spoof of the song "Oops, I Did It Again" by Britney Spears that one or both of you can sing when something is forgotten. Singing and laughing together can help you acknowledge what happened and reset the mood.

There aren't any magical solutions that will make someone remember or take away all the frustration you might feel when something has been forgotten. But knowing how to mitigate the damage when forgetfulness happens goes a long way toward strengthening your relationship.

Copy That!

Even if you think your partner with ADHD heard what you said, it's helpful to make a habit of asking them to repeat what they understood you to say. This avoids miscommunication. Here's an example of how this might sound:

PARTNER A: *Can you repeat back what you heard?*

PARTNER B: *You made my lunch today.*

PARTNER A: *Yes! And it is in the fridge. Would it be helpful to write yourself a reminder?*

PARTNER B: *Yes, thank you. I'm looking forward to enjoying your amazing food!*

▶ TIP Stay positive! If your partner can't repeat back what they heard, let them know what they missed and thank them for repeating it back. If you get frustrated, this strategy won't work. Celebrate that you have an opportunity to straighten out any miscommunication before it actually causes a problem! This strengthens the relationship pillars of praise and acknowledgment.

THE UPSIDE

Having a weak working memory means the partner with ADHD tends to also forget about the times they may have been hurt or disappointed. Because they don't get stuck in the details, this contributes to their spontaneity and positivity. This is a wonderful gift for any relationship: the balance of letting go and having fun.

Task List

As a team, create a task list of all the chores that need to get done to operate your household. Divvy the tasks up. Each partner can begin by choosing the tasks they feel are the easiest for them to do. Generally speaking, an ADHD brain will do better with tasks that can become part of their daily routine—for example, washing the dishes, which needs to be done daily, as opposed to taking out the trash every few days. Discuss the other tasks on your list that haven't been assigned yet and agree on how best to divvy them up.

Put this task list in a common area of the house as a daily reminder. You can also get an app such as Trello where you can add tasks and assign responsibility with reminders. Schedule weekly or biweekly meetings to review the tasks and plan for the next ones. Remember to praise each other for the things you both did well. If there are any challenges, use your teamwork skills to think of ways to overcome them. After the meeting, do something fun and rewarding.

Remember that it takes practice to master new strategies. Even if this fails the first few times, keep trying!

▶ TIP Speak in positives, not negatives. Instead of saying, "Don't forget," say, "Please remember." This is a better reminder of the desired behavior. For example, if you say, "Don't run," the brain has to think about what it needs to do instead. "Walk, please" is a more effective statement because it reinforces the desired action: walking.

- ADHD brains have to overcome a lot of challenges, like distraction and weak working memory, to remember tasks and conversations.

- Frustration from a weak working memory can cause conflicts within a relationship when the Five Relationship Pillars are not present.

- The non-ADHD partner may get burned out and resent doing tasks that their partner forgets to start or complete.

- Using the Five Relationship Pillars when exploring effective strategies sets up a neurodiverse couple for success.

CHAPTER SEVEN

The Disorganization Is Real

E veryone has a different tolerance for clutter. When there's a big discrepancy, it can be a source of frequent arguments and stress. Sometimes, what one partner needs directly conflicts with what the other wants. In a neurodiverse relationship, the partner with ADHD often needs clutter as visual reminders to function well. This is usually the opposite of what their neurotypical partner needs: an organized space to function well. All Five Relationship Pillars are necessary to figure out a way for both partners to live comfortably together. What makes sense to one brain may not make any sense to the other brain, creating a battle of two organization systems with no winner.

CLUTTER, CLUTTER, EVERYWHERE

Most clients with ADHD I see say they don't mind their cluttered spaces. Many say it's easier to find things in their "mess" as opposed to after their partner has "organized" it. They don't understand the point of spending time putting things away because it doesn't matter to them. They prefer to prioritize other activities over straightening up after themselves. If their neurotypical partner needs a clean home to feel at ease, this can cause a lot of stress for the ADHD brain. They may attempt to keep the home more organized but feel constantly stressed out by the prospect of having to keep it up. They also start feeling as if their partner is always disappointed in them or looking for the one thing they didn't do. Let's take a look from an ADHD perspective:

> Greg wanted to make his wife, Liz, happy. He took a day off from work to surprise her by straightening up around the house and doing some household maintenance. He waited with excitement for her to get home that day so he could see the huge smile on her face. Instead, Liz didn't even notice his effort. In fact, she immediately mentioned that he had left the garage door open and it looked like a disaster. Greg was devasted. He pointed out that he had fixed the hinges on the kitchen cabinet and then felt ridiculed when Liz said, "Finally. I've been asking you to do that for months." Greg felt a burst of anger and resentment. It was unfair that all the stuff he did didn't seem to matter. He took hours out of his day doing all the chores Liz had assigned to him just to make her happy. He began thinking how selfish she was because she only noticed her own efforts.

ADHD Relationships

Everyone has a different level of tolerance for messes, which is why this is often an issue in relationships. Being prone to clutter doesn't mean someone has ADHD, of course, and there are many common strategies to help people stay organized. However, these common strategies are not designed for the ADHD brain, so using them can just add to the frustration. Here are three reasons why clutter and ADHD go hand in hand and why common strategies are not as effective for the partner with ADHD:

Weak working memory. Clutter provides visual reminders of things to do and where things are. Leaving things out is easier than figuring out an organizational system that would hide stuff from sight. "Out of sight, out of mind" applies to the ADHD brain, making it harder for them to find things.

Weak organization and planning. The steps required to organize things and put them away can be too overwhelming for someone with ADHD. It's usually easier to leave things out in the open, where they can see them.

Growing up in clutter. Since ADHD has a large genetic component, there is a good chance the partner with ADHD grew up in a household that was not organized and therefore didn't get much instruction on how to effectively put things away.

When clutter messes up your relationship, the relationship pillars cease to exist. The most important pillars to focus on are acknowledgment and praise when navigating how to organize stuff.

STRATEGIES

Neurodiverse couples need to figure out effective strategies to avoid making clutter a source of conflict in their relationship. If possible, hiring a professional organizer who specializes in ADHD can save a lot of time and energy. Other strategies that are suitable for an ADHD brain may be just what the relationship needs.

Space to Be Me

If you need a place to dump your stuff and not deal with it until you're ready, arrange with your partner to set aside a space in your home that can be yours alone to keep however you like. Perhaps you have an extra room that can be yours or maybe something smaller like a particular closet or storage bench. It's okay for things to be messy in that area if it works for you. Having a protected space allows your brain to organize your stuff in a way that helps you be productive and at ease.

▶ TIP The area that's set aside for the partner with ADHD needs to be easy to get to or this strategy won't work. For instance, an attic that you can only get to by ladder wouldn't be an option.

Keep It Simple

When organizing your home, a key principle to keep in mind is that less is more. The more steps it takes to put away an item, the more chances are that it won't be put away. For example, if you put jackets in an upstairs closet, you have to walk up the stairs, go to the closet, and hang up a jacket. This provides ample time to be distracted along the way to the closet, increasing the chances of dropping the jacket in a place that will be hard to find later. Having a coat stand near the front door would be more effective since it requires fewer steps.

Visual cues like the coat stand can help you remember to put things away without needing to use your working memory or going very far out of your way. Here are two other examples:

• Mount a key holder by the door. It will act as a visual reminder to put your keys away when you get home.
• Place a mail bin by the front door to increase the chances you will use it instead of leaving the mail on the counter.

"WE LIVE IN A MESS"

Many neurotypical partners become stressed when their home is in disarray and unorganized and they can't find anything. The environment can actually feel chaotic to their nervous system. Over time, living in a messy house can take a toll on their mental health. To try to avoid the mess and disorganization, they usually turn to one or more of these strategies:

They regularly pick up after their partner to keep things organized. Someone with ADHD can create more clutter than a neurotypical adult. When children are involved, picking up after everyone can become a full-time job—especially if a child has ADHD as well.

They coach their partner on various strategies that work for them. Because these strategies are typically designed for neurotypical people, they feel frustrated when their partner isn't able to use them.

They continually explain how important it is for them to live in a clean home. Even if their partner tries for a time to make them happy, they just can't keep it up.

When these strategies don't work, the non-ADHD partner may feel unappreciated and alone. Let's take a look from the non-ADHD perspective:

> Liz felt bewildered that Greg didn't notice how messy their house was. It didn't make sense to her how Greg was not bothered by this at all. It stressed her out when Greg would leave her unopened mail in different rooms. She was frustrated that simple tasks seemed so hard for him. She had explained how to wipe down the counter multiple times but on Greg's nights to do it, it was always left undone. It really just seemed like Greg was a tornado that managed to leave lights on, things all over the place, and drawers open wherever he went. Liz felt like she had two toddlers in the house.

She was anxious and stressed by the stuff everywhere yet was too exhausted to pick up after her husband and a toddler. She felt bad because she snapped at Greg more often when she was stressed. She felt helpless because nothing changed. She had explained multiple times that cleaning up and staying mess-free were important to her. Why was it so hard for Greg to put things away?

ADHD Relationships

After telling their partner with ADHD numerous times how important a clutter-free home is to them to no avail, the neurotypical partner starts believing that their partner doesn't care about their needs. However, the continued clutter is a reflection of their partner's weak executive function skills in attention and organization and planning—not on how much they care about their partner.

Because someone with ADHD can become easily distracted, they tend to leave things in random places. This becomes amplified when kids are around, as they are interrupting their parent's focus all the time. Items tend to be left out of the fridge and not put away. Coffee mugs are repeatedly lost and found in the morning. Remote controls wind up in bathrooms. And so on. This can be incredibly frustrating for the neurotypical partner who has a system in place. What's more, a weak working memory can make it challenging for someone with ADHD to remember where things go.

The relationship pillars of acknowledgment, praise, and positive acceptance are especially necessary here. As explained earlier, clutter can actually be helpful for the ADHD brain, which has developed its own system to make up for a weak working memory. What calms the neurotypical partner down (a clutter-free home) may stress the partner with ADHD out because they may be more forgetful without their system (a clutter-filled home) of visual cues to remind them.

For putting away an object, the following executive functions need to happen:

> **Attention.** They need to notice that an item that is out of place, focus on putting it away, and not be distracted by other stimuli before the task is completed.

Planning and organization. Knowing how to organize a household directly relates to this skill. It takes planning and organizational focus to know where things would be best placed and easily found. It also takes planning to know how to prioritize all the tasks one needs to accomplish.

Self-control. Since putting things away isn't fun, this requires restraining oneself from doing a more enjoyable activity, like watching TV or going out with friends.

This is a lot of work for someone who doesn't have strong executive function skills in these areas. Since most neurodiverse couples don't understand how challenging these tasks are for someone with ADHD, they aren't able to acknowledge and appreciate the effort that is being made.

STRATEGIES

It is important for the non-ADHD partner to remember that they are asking their partner to do something challenging because it matters to them. Acknowledging and recognizing when their partner makes an effort to declutter supports their goal of having an organized house. They must avoid dismissing or minimizing their ADHD partner's efforts, which includes saying things like "Well, it's about time" or "Why do I need to praise you for what you are supposed to do?" Those types of statements effectively tell the ADHD brain it shouldn't bother making the effort because it's not good enough. The opposite strategy is what's needed to motivate them.

Praise, Praise, PRAISE!

Pay attention to when your partner straightens up around the house or puts something away in the right place. Praise their efforts and express your appreciation. For example, you might say something like: "This is *amazing*! The remote is in its place! This helps me so much. I love it when I am able to sit down and relax in front of the TV instead of stressing over where the remote might be." Or "I feel so relaxed and calm now that things are put away. I know you did this for me. It makes me so grateful that you put in the effort to do this."

If your partner did happen to "miss a spot" and you want to say something, make sure you start and end with recognizing and appreciating what they did do well. Aim for a five-to-one ratio of praise to improvement. Remember, high reward (praise) motivates the ADHD brain to function better, whereas negative reinforcement (criticism and anger) makes it want to disengage.

Labeled Bins

Having labeled bins in your home can be an effective system for both types of brains in a neurodiverse relationship. The labels provide a visual reminder for the partner with ADHD, which tells them to store things in the bin after use. For example, you might label the bins "remote controls" or "keys" or "office supplies."

Keep the system simple and close to the action area. For instance, the bin labeled "remote controls" would be placed closer to the couch or television and "keys" would be closer to the front door.

Placing the bins in a bookcase and/or on shelves can keep the house looking clean and organized, which is a win for both brains!

> **THE UPSIDE**
> When a neurodiverse couple uses effective strategies to keep their home organized, thereby reducing conflict, fun and connection can become more of a priority. The ADHD brain is great at making that happen. Both types of brain balance each other out for a well-rounded relationship.

Clean Sweep

As discussed, routines and schedules help the ADHD brain complete challenging tasks like tidying up. This exercise is intended to help both of you (and your children if you have any) get into the habit of tidying up every day. Since it's often more important to the non-ADHD partner to have an organized home, that partner is responsible for setting up the routine and providing positive reinforcement. It will take a few weeks before it becomes a habit, so the non-ADHD partner can expect to be the leader in this for about a month.

Pick a time that works for both of you to tidy up the house. Before bed or after dinner may be convenient times. If you have kids, get them involved in this as well. Set an alarm to go off at this time every day.

When the daily alarm sounds, assign each person an area of the house to tidy up.

Set a timer for 10 minutes and see who can tidy up their area the fastest. Make it fun. Play songs that get you moving!

When the timer sounds, celebrate! Do a silly dance, high five, or group hug to recognize that each person is contributing to the home.

- Neurodiverse couples need effective strategies that work for both brains to keep clutter from being an ongoing source of conflict.

- Adults with ADHD may be using clutter to support a weak working memory; a room or area of their own that they can keep however they want can help satisfy this need.

- When the non-ADHD partner praises their partner for their help, their partner is more likely to help them in the future because the ADHD brain is motivated by praise.

- Making tidying up the home more like a game can motivate everyone in the home to pitch in!

CHAPTER EIGHT

The Parent-Child Dynamic

C hildren often struggle with seemingly simple household tasks and responsibilities because they are still in the process of developing their executive function skills. Their struggles are similar to those experienced by an adult with ADHD. As such, neurotypical partners may find themselves resorting to parenting techniques. This unhelpful strategy causes the relationship to evolve into a parent-child dynamic instead of primary partners. Given that your relationship is between two adults, this dynamic doesn't feel good to either of you. This chapter offers strategies based on the Five Relationship Pillars to change your relationship into two interdependent adults working as a team.

"I FEEL LIKE A CHILD"

Even though adults with ADHD and children with ADHD confront similar challenges such as time management, completing tasks, orderliness, and emotional outbursts, adults with ADHD go on to have very successful lives, especially in their careers. Most likely they were also able to manage their life well enough before they got into a relationship. So, when their non-ADHD partner starts using parenting strategies to "help" deal with some of their challenges, it can feel condescending and disrespectful.

Partners with ADHD commonly complain that they are being treated like children; they are told what to do, deemed untrustworthy, and even worse, are punished when they don't do things "right." Adults with ADHD reject the idea that they are not functional because their life was fully functioning before they were in a relationship as well as outside the relationship. Here's how this looks from an ADHD perspective:

> Austin was beyond annoyed with his wife, Becka. She was controlling and treated him like a child. He told her how her rules made him feel incompetent and untrusted, to which she would reply, "I'll stop when you behave like an adult." This enraged him. Sure, he forgot things occasionally and sometimes was late to pick up the kids from school, but her response was extreme. It killed any chemistry or attraction and made him wonder why he put up with such controlling behavior. He could leave his shoes wherever he wanted because it was his house, too. He oscillated from rage to sadness. He did love Becka, but he didn't know how their relationship had turned so angry and bitter.

ADHD Relationships

When the partner with ADHD feels controlled and/or like a failure, it can lead to intense fights. This is because none of the Five Relationship Pillars are present in this dynamic, making it an unhealthy environment for the person with ADHD. It leaves both partners working against each other. Of course, the non-ADHD partner isn't trying to create a negative environment and generally wants to be helpful. But this often includes using parentlike strategies because that is all they know. Since parenting strategies can be more harmful than helpful to an ADHD brain, the resentment, fights, and disengagement become commonplace.

Here are some of the unhelpful strategies neurotypical partners may use to change their partner's behavior:

- Criticizing what their partner is doing and/or focusing on the negative.
- Comparing their partner to others to help motivate them to change. They often use phrases like "If everyone else can do it, why can't you?" and "Even a child could do this!"
- Shaming them by making personality statements based on their behavior: "You are lazy, stupid, an idiot, a bad parent, etc."
- Telling them their intentions: "You obviously don't care, or you would do it."
- Controlling or restricting their participation in activities.
- Punishing them by withholding affection, money, activities, etc.

Normally, people employ these strategies because they're the methods they learned from others at home or at school when they were growing up. These strategies use negative reinforcement (motivating a change in behavior by avoiding a negative consequence), which, as you now understand, isn't effective for the ADHD brain. Using the wrong strategies contributes to this negative cycle.

STRATEGIES

The parent-child dynamic can be solved by incorporating the Five Relationship Pillars into all interactions. For most couples, the easiest pillar and the one that can have an immediate impact on the relationship is praise. The following strategies are designed to help you know what kind of praise (positive reinforcement) is best for the partner with ADHD in your relationship.

Biggest Fan

Think about the times you've felt supported when you were struggling. What did the person do or say? Use this example to generate a list to share with your partner of what your brain needs to hear when you are modifying your behavior to reduce the conflict in your relationship. Common helpful statements for you to hear might sound like:

"I see that you are trying really hard and that it was important for you to accomplish your goal, even if it didn't work."

"This one mess-up doesn't define you. You are such a good person who cares so much. We will get through this."

"I appreciate how you work hard to do things for our family, even if they don't go as planned. Know that I love you for you, and not just because of the tasks you complete."

"There are so many good things that you give to us and the world, and those are worth so much more to me than this one thing."

If you feel like a failure, your ADHD "brakes" may fail, leading to an emotional outburst. However, getting your partner's reassurance in the form of statements like these can help your brain get back on track.

▶ **TIP** If you normally motivate yourself by telling yourself how horrible you are, learn more effective motivation strategies by revisiting chapter 3.

Daily Affirmations

Daily affirmations can help you and your partner break the parent-child dynamic. Spend 5 to 10 minutes every morning for a partner chat. During this time, each of you will share three positive affirmations regarding the other person or your relationship. You can look back at your relationship goals from chapter 2 as a guideline for creating your affirmations. Here are some affirmations to get you started:

- "I commit to growing and learning with you, even if it is tough."
- "I seek to understand you and accept your point of view."
- "I acknowledge that we are in a tough time in our relationship, and I will work with you as a team to overcome it."
- "Our relationship provides love, stability, and acceptance for me, and I am grateful for that."

THE NON-ADHD PARTNER
"I FEEL LIKE THE PARENT"

Typically, the non-ADHD partner tries a variety of techniques before resorting to "parenting" their partner. Many neurotypical partners wait patiently for their partner to change. They refrain from saying anything because they're afraid to sound like a nag, hurt their partner's feelings, or cause relationship conflict. The partner with ADHD has no idea how hard their partner is trying to respect them as an adult and support them by not intervening.

However, after experiencing the consequences of their partner's weak executive function skills time and time again, the neurotypical partner feels more and more responsible and burdened. For example, if their partner impulsively spends their joint funds, it can disrupt the couple's budget and impact their ability to pay their monthly bills. Eventually, it becomes easier for the neurotypical partner to avoid this entirely by controlling the finances or their partner's access to credit cards or debit cards. They may not like doing this but often feel helpless to prevent the negative effects of their partner's impulsive decisions otherwise.

As you've learned, weak executive functioning skills don't provide the ADHD brain with good "brakes," which can lead to big crashes. Since the non-ADHD partner has likely witnessed this many times, they try to prevent future crashes by imposing rules and setting limits. Here's how this looks from a non-ADHD perspective:

> Setting limits for Austin exhausted Becka. She hated having to do it and felt it was unfair that she even needed to. She had tried everything she could think of: being patient, encouraging, complaining, and even begging Austin to get his act together. She assumed he would start being more responsible when he became a dad. Initially, she worried that he would think she was being annoying, but she grew tired of cleaning up Austin's messes, literally and figuratively. It was easier for her to manage everything to avoid getting dragged into one of Austin's big consequences. She resented her husband for making her feel like she had another child instead of a partner. Her patience had grown thin, and it became harder for her not to explode at him. To top it off, the situation killed her sex drive; she was exhausted from managing all the responsibilities of a home and family.

ADHD Relationships

It often seems easier and more efficient for the neurotypical partner to do the various tasks that need to get done, and they fall into the habit of overfunctioning. For example, even though they'd like their partner to clean up after dinner, they know that it will take twice as long for them to get it done at the expense of couple time or help putting the kids to bed. In their mind, it's just easier for them to do it. However, this can take a toll on them if they're always the one managing things and don't have any downtime to have some fun. If the partner with ADHD is the parent the kids love to play with, the neurotypical partner may feel that it's unfair that they never get to be the "fun parent." Without realizing it, when they feel burdened by managing most of the relationship and home responsibilities, many non-ADHD partners stop nurturing the Five Relationship Pillars. Here is how it goes:

Praise: It becomes harder to praise any effort by the partner with ADHD because any effort feels insufficient to the amount of support the non-ADHD partner actually needs.

Acknowledgment: The ADHD symptoms become merged with the ADHD partner's identity and there's no acknowledgment of the individual.

Games: Relaxing and engaging in fun, playful activities takes a backseat to taking care of household responsibilities.

Growth mindset: Adopting an attitude of "I have to do it all" effectively stops the relationship from growing.

Positive acceptance: With built-up frustration and resentment, holding one's partner in a positive regard becomes difficult.

Nurturing the Five Relationship Pillars takes energy and commitment. If the non-ADHD partner already feels exhausted, it's easy to stop investing in the relationship pillars and resort to complaining, nagging, and punishing, but that's not going to help the relationship.

STRATEGIES

The first strategy helps the overfunctioning partner delegate some tasks to their partner. Although it can be difficult, this is possible when the neurotypical partner is willing to let go of some expectations around how things need to get done. The second strategy addresses the resentment that builds when one partner feels like they are doing more than their fair share and doesn't feel acknowledged or appreciated.

Wiggle Room

Think about some of the things you normally take care of that you can delegate to your partner. Ideally, these areas won't have a big impact on you. Write them down and share them with your partner. Plan to be okay with how your partner manages the task. Here are some ideas to get you started:

• Plan a date night.
• Do their own laundry. (If you are okay with waiting for clean clothes, you can ask them to do your laundry as well.)
• Put away any toys left out by young children at the end of the day.
• Change the oil in the car. (Since the "change oil" icon comes on in the car, this is a good reminder for someone with ADHD.)
• Load, run, and unload the dishwasher.

▶ **TIP Make sure your partner has 100 percent ownership of the task. For example, loading, running, and unloading the dishwasher is a complete task. If you say, "You unload the dishwasher, and I will load the dishwasher," your ability to load the dishwasher is dependent on your partner's completing their part. Avoid this by handing over the whole responsibility.**

Biggest Fan

Make a list of the areas where you feel unappreciated, or tasks you do around the house and for your family that go unnoticed. Think of what you want to hear to make it feel like your contributions are being valued. Generate a list to share with your partner. Some common statements that are helpful for the non-ADHD partner to hear include:

"I know that you are doing so much for this family, and I appreciate it. It takes a lot of work to keep a house running, and you are doing a great job."

"Thank you for keeping our home clean so we have a nice place to relax. I know this is important to you and challenging for me."

"Thanks for making sure the kids get into a camp. I know I would wait until the last minute when all the camps are full. I love that you think of these things in advance."

"Thanks for planning trips and fun outings. I recognize this as an investment in our relationship, and I appreciate it."

Knowing that your partner appreciates all the effort you put in around your home and for your relationship can go a long way toward easing some feelings of resentment. Encourage them to share these acknowledgments with you.

THE UPSIDE
When a couple recognizes the strengths that each type of brain brings to the relationship, deep admiration and appreciation blossom. When all Five Relationship Pillars create the foundation of your relationship, your neurodiversity is precisely what makes your relationship robust, resilient, and balanced.

Relationship Connection

It's time to play a game—and who doesn't like a good game of connect-the-boxes? Here's the board:

Tell the story of how you fell in love.	When is the last time you felt appreciated by your partner?	Re-create your most passionate kiss	What are the qualities that attracted you to your partner?
Imagine your relationship in 10 years. What do you want it to look like?	When was the last time you overstepped your role as a partner? What would you have liked to do differently?	What are the strengths your partner brings to the relationship?	What does your partner do better than you that you appreciate?
Where do you want to grow as a couple and what would that look like in five years?	When was the last time you were accountable and apologized first after a fight?	What is a favorite memory as a couple?	When did you show respect to your partner by letting them do things their way?
Describe the last time you felt like you and your partner were equal partners working together.	When do you feel the most loved and connected to your partner?	Name three things your partner has done that made your relationship or home better.	Name something your partner does that supports an area you struggle with.

How to play:

The first player chooses any box and completes the task. Once completed, they put their initial in the box. The second player takes a turn. When you have four boxes in a row, column, or diagonally, collect your prize. The other player can complete tasks until they also get to collect a prize.

Suggestions for prizes:

Make 10 or more coupons or gift certificates for things you know will make each of you happy. Coupons can be redeemed at any time. The other person must fulfill the coupon within a set time frame, such as 24 hours. (You can change the time limit if needed, but the shorter the time, the better.) Here are some ideas to get you started:

- Do the dishes (wash, dry, and put away)
- Spend 15 minutes cuddling
- Pick the movie/show to watch
- Foot massage

- Put the kids to bed
- Cook dinner
- Share how much you love me
- Long hug
- Lots of kisses

▶ **TIP** If there is too much resentment between you to play a game, it is a sign to get professional assistance. Changing habits and dynamics can be tough, and getting support can help get your relationship to a place that feels good again.

- The issues that occur in a neurodiverse relationship can result in a parent-child dynamic, which harms the relationship.

- When this dynamic is present, the partner with ADHD resents being treated like a child, and the non-ADHD partner overfunctions, often to exhaustion, to prevent negative consequences.

- The type of negative reinforcement a parent or teacher might use on a child is not effective or helpful for an adult with ADHD.

- Focusing on the Five Relationship Pillars can change the parent-child dynamic in a neurodiverse relationship and bring it to new heights.

CHAPTER NINE

Missing the Point

Stigma, myths, and shame still surround mental health issues, even in today's society. This is mostly due to the lack of public health education around mental health. Some people may need to overcome faulty preconceptions before they are willing to seek help. This chapter explains the challenges that many people face when considering whether to seek professional counseling, and how the Five Relationship Pillars can combat the stigma and fear that may be associated with it.

"THERE IS NOTHING WRONG WITH ME"

Many adults with ADHD today grew up in an era when mental issues were stigmatized, especially in school. They may be reluctant to seek help, as the stigma has not yet been completely eradicated. Contributing to the issue is a lack of public policies educating people on when to seek professional help. As is the case with physical health, earlier interventions have a better prognosis. It's impossible to know why someone would choose not to get treatment for their ADHD, but these are some of the reasons I've heard:

- "I don't want to be seen as broken."
- "If I am diagnosed, it will mean everything is my fault."
- "I am fine and resent being told I am not fine."
- "If I see a therapist it means there is something wrong with me."
- "I am not crazy or want to kill myself." (Believing that is a requirement to get help.)
- "I don't want to lose myself." (Fear of being changed by therapy and/or medicine.)
- "They will force me to take medicine."
- "It feels overwhelming."
- "I am scared. What if something is really wrong?"
- "I am not a child."

This is how it might sound from an ADHD perspective:

> I am fine. There is nothing wrong with me. All couples have challenges, and we just need to work through them. My partner is trying to blame all our problems on me, which is not accurate. I have managed to stay alive, pay my bills, and have held a job my whole adult life. Why would I pay someone to help me when I don't need any help?

Even if the partner with ADHD is open to therapy, finding a therapist who treats adult ADHD, is a good fit, accepts your insurance, and has availability requires a number of mundane tasks. This can be time-consuming and overwhelming. Calling numerous therapists only to find out they do not have openings or don't accept your insurance can be defeating. It is important to keep trying and work as a team so neither partner feels overly burdened by the task. If you are seeking a psychiatrist, be aware that it can take up to three months for an appointment, so if possible, get on a waitlist.

ADHD Relationships

If the Five Relationship Pillars are not present, discussions around treatment for ADHD can cause conflict between the partners. They may disagree on the seriousness of the problem and how to fix it (treatment versus nontreatment). This goes against the pillar of positive acceptance. Each partner in the relationship has a right to choose whether to seek treatment for a problem and/or take medication for it. The Five Relationship Pillars provide a healthy supportive environment that can make it easier for anyone, whether or not they have ADHD, to get support. Here are some ways each pillar can reduce some of the common barriers:

- A growth mindset encourages you to support each other as individuals and as a couple in moving forward in your relationship.
- Positive acceptance means that no matter any diagnosis, you are both good and worthwhile people.
- Acknowledgment of the stigma around ADHD can make it less challenging to seek help.
- The act of giving each other praise for being courageous and making the effort to do something hard is the encouragement you each might need.
- Celebrating the hard stuff and making space for games reassures you both that your relationship is resilient and can be rewarding.

STRATEGIES

The partner with ADHD may not know if they will find professional support helpful. They also might not be sure how to talk about seeking help with their neurotypical partner. In some cases, they may feel that their non-ADHD partner is pressuring them to get therapy when they do not want to. Both of the following strategies are helpful conversation starters around the idea of professional support.

Make a List

If you are against the idea of getting professional support for your ADHD or you are simply unsure of why it might be a good idea, it can help to think about other types of professional you might get, for instance:

- A personal trainer
- A tutor
- A teacher/professor
- A yoga/art/dance class instructor
- A workshop leader

Getting help from these people would be seen as an investment in yourself—not a sign of weakness. Reflect on why you think it would be okay to receive support in other areas but not in the area of your mental health. On a blank sheet of paper, write down all the reasons you can think of. Use this list to share your perspective with your partner.

What I Hear You Say

If your partner is asking you to seek treatment for your ADHD, think about how your brain is interpreting their request. Write your interpretations on a blank piece of paper. Some common interpretations sound like:

"You blame me for everything."

"You don't like me and see me as worthless."

"You do not want to be accountable for your part of our problems."

Share your list with your partner. Remind your partner that this is what your brain hears and not necessarily what your partner said. Brainstorm different ways your partner can communicate with you so that your brain interprets their words as an act of love and care. Use the Five Relationship Pillars and your relationship goals (page 33) as a guide for your brainstorming session.

THE NON-ADHD PARTNER
"THEY'RE IN DENIAL"

Sometimes the neurotypical partner thinks that if their partner with ADHD got treatment, all their relationship problems would go away. However, both partners' behavior is more than likely contributing to the issues the couple is facing. The non-ADHD partner may also interpret their partner's refusal to seek treatment as a sign that they don't care about the relationship or their partner's well-being.

Trying to fix the problem and expecting both partners to interpret events the same way ignores the Five Relationship Pillars, which can create even more conflict. Although the neurotypical partner may be coming from a helpful place, they may be communicating their message in a way their partner finds unhelpful, which contributes to the issues the couple is facing. Here's how this might sound from a non-ADHD perspective:

> I feel so helpless. I know my partner has ADHD, so am I just supposed to put up with everything? I cannot take their mood swings and angry outbursts. I love my partner, but I've hit my limit. They refuse to see a therapist, so what else can I do? When things are good, they are so amazing. But when it is bad, it feels unbearable. I hate being torn because I do understand this isn't their fault. At the same time, they won't get help to make the situation easier for me!

ADHD Relationships

Author of *The ADHD Effect on Marriage* Melissa Orlov explains that treatment is part of the solution for both partners. The non-ADHD partner will need to learn new skills and recover from any issues they may have experienced due to the stress and conflict in the neurodiverse relationship. Focusing on which person is the root of the problem only creates a divide; partners need to feel like a team. As explained in chapter 1, both partners need to learn new skills to effectively communicate with each other. They will need to work on using the Five Relationship Pillars as their foundation to overcome challenges.

It is fine to acknowledge that ADHD has affected you; it's how you express it that makes a huge difference in your relationship. Here's an example of how to talk about your concerns using the Five Relationship Pillars:

"I want you to know that I love you as you are, and I don't want to change you." (Positive Acceptance)

"I am sharing this idea out of a place of love, care, and desire to improve our relationship, as we committed to in our relationship goals." (Growth Mindset)

"I am concerned that some of our issues keep coming up because we do not have the right skills. It would be very meaningful for me if we go to therapy as a couple, and individually, so that we can learn how to support each other. I understand that therapy is something you don't want to do, but going with me shows me how much you care about me and value my opinion, even if it is different from your own." (Praise and Acknowledgment)

"You don't need to answer right away. I know this is a big ask." (Acknowledgment)

"Thank you for honoring our relationship goals and having these tough conversations, I know we are an amazing couple and want to prioritize us in a way that feels good to us both." (Praise and Growth Mindset)

STRATEGIES

The following strategies focus on how the non-ADHD partner can get the support they need and communicate to their partner why treatment is important to them individually and as a couple.

Get Support

Even if your partner chooses not to pursue therapy, you can still get a coach or therapist to support you. A coach or therapist can help you build upon the strategies you've learned in this book. This includes effectively communicating with your partner while also helping you take care of yourself by setting boundaries for a healthier relationship.

Learning new skills and modeling the growth mindset for your partner can also make going to therapy less scary or strange for them.

What Couples Therapy Means to Me

Why is going to couples therapy important to you? Think about this for a while, and once you have some solid ideas, list all your reasons on a sheet of paper. Consider how your relationship goals and the Five Relationship Pillars align with getting therapy. Share your reasons with your partner to begin an open and honest dialogue around this idea.

To help you get started, here are some reasons other couples find going to couples therapy meaningful to their relationship:

"It shows that we both value this relationship and are committed to learning and growing together."

"It shows me that you value my thoughts and beliefs."

"It shows me that you support me even if our opinions are different."

"It shows me that you are brave and will go above and beyond for this relationship."

"It makes me feel safe that we have professional support and are not in this alone."

THE UPSIDE

Getting support can put your neurodiverse relationship back on the path toward a joyful, fulfilling partnership. At their best, neurodiverse couples freely express their love, have lots of fun together, and thrive in life. When neurodiverse couples navigate through challenges as a team, they come out stronger and more connected. Other couples often aspire to have a relationship just like theirs!

There Is Help

This is a fun activity with a visual reminder to help you stay in a growth mindset. For starters, make a pair of "growth mindset" hats. You'll need two pieces of construction paper, markers, and tape. On the construction paper, jot down the benefits of learning and growing, individually and together. Here are some ideas to get you started:

- Knowledge is power
- Strength comes from learning
- Sharing is caring

Roll the paper into a cone and tape the edges to make a hat. Make sure the words are facing out. Wear these hats as you complete the rest of the exercise.

Together, complete the following table by rating each challenge on a scale of 1 to 10, with 10 having the biggest negative impact, or highest cost. (By the way, these challenges aren't exclusive to ADHD. One or both of you may want to improve in a certain area.)

CHALLENGE	COST TO RELATIONSHIP	COST TO PARTNER A	COST TO PARTNER B
Clutter			
Criticism			
Distraction			
Emotional regulation			
Memory			
Overfunctioning			
Perfectionism			
Self-esteem			
Time management			
Other:			

Look at the areas with the biggest negative impact on each of you and the relationship. These are the areas you will want to focus on improving. Choose one or two areas to work on first, while keeping the others in mind for the future.

Next, explore the various types of support that may be available to you individually and as a couple. Together, think of at least one benefit and one drawback for each type of therapy. Jot down some key words in the following table to represent the benefits and drawbacks.

TYPE OF SUPPORT	BENEFITS	DRAWBACKS
Couples therapy		
Executive skills class		
Housekeeper		
Individual coaching		
Individual therapy		
Medication		
Professional organizer		
Support group		
Virtual or personal assistant		
Other:		

Once you've completed the written part of this exercise, reexamine the evidence. Can the biggest challenge(s) you identified be helped by one of the types of support? If so, discuss getting the help of a professional as well as the steps of how to do that. Discuss who will be responsible for researching and reaching out to professionals. Take notes to jog your memories later. Once you're all done with that, CELEBRATE! Honor that this exercise was hard work, but now it's time to have some fun! Do something you both enjoy.

CHAPTER 9 TAKEAWAYS

- Focusing on just one partner getting treatment can take away from the Five Relationship Pillars, creating a negative environment for both.

- The Five Relationship Pillars provide a safe foundation upon which you can bravely try new things, such as therapy.

- It is important for both partners to share their concerns and opinions about getting outside help. Both must respect each person's autonomy in making medical choices for their mind and body.

- Other ways to get support aside from therapy include things like hiring a housekeeper or getting an assistant.

CHAPTER TEN

The Journey Ahead

G etting out of negative cycles is tough. Once a couple is in one, it can feel like a daunting task to change behaviors. Hopefully, this book has helped you realize that much of your relationship conflict stems from not knowing that your brains work differently and that you're using the wrong communication strategies. The good news is that by focusing on the Five Relationship Pillars and effective communication strategies for someone with ADHD, the toxic cycle can be broken. The earlier you start, the easier it is. You don't have to wait until things feel really bad to make a change. Every couple's journey is different, but this chapter will lay out the common milestones for the road ahead.

REBUILDING TRUST

First, congratulate yourself for reading this book. It shows that you care and are invested in your relationship. I hope that both of you have come to realize that you've been making an effort to improve your relationship, which perhaps had been going unnoticed.

It is time to try out your new "language" by changing how you communicate using the Five Relationship Pillars. This will take effort, patience, and perseverance from both of you. It will also take trust in each other to change habits and behaviors that feel comfortable to you, because the process takes time before it becomes your new norm. Celebrate failing and learning as you embark on strengthening your relationship. Together, explore if the new strategies in this book are helpful. If not, you are learning what doesn't work for you!

Both of you will have moments of stress that will bring out previously unhelpful behaviors due to your ingrained neural pathways. This can cause many partners to give up practicing the new strategies because they think the other isn't trying if they resort to old patterns. This is where trust comes in. You have to trust the process and recognize that it will be harder at the beginning. Just like learning a new language, it can be frustrating not being able to communicate as well as you do in your native language. However, the reward is worth it when you master it. This is also why a coach or therapist can be a great resource when learning your new communication skills.

I'll Grow with You

Learning a new relationship language takes practice. Although the Five Relationship Pillars may seem easy to understand, it takes awareness and effort to use them every day in your relationship. Get two notebooks, one for each partner. For the next two weeks, write down an act you did that day to strengthen each of the pillars. Spend a few minutes doing this, and then share it with each other. Here's an example:

Praise: I celebrated you for doing the dishes.

Acknowledgment: I verbally acknowledged that you organized a playdate for our kid. I know that is work and I appreciate that you think about and do these things.

Games: I made sure we had laughter and silliness after dinner today.

Growth Mindset: I used the "I Failed" strategy when I left the milk out overnight.

Positive Acceptance: I respected you as a person by focusing on a behavior that was bothering me and reminded you that I love you as you are.

These acts can be simple and small. Set yourself up for success. If you forgot to do one and can't think of something in the moment, take a bow and say, "I failed!" and your partner will clap and say, "You learned!" It will take time to cultivate the skill to include the Five Relationship Pillars daily. The bonus is that you will have a visual reminder of how each of you is working on the relationship. These small changes over time will have a positive impact on your relationship.

THE PERKS

With any new skill, there is a benefit and a drawback. This is true for all people, and can be helpful in relationships when you see the benefit that something provides along with the challenge. Now that you've read about some of the challenges neurodiverse couples face, let's take a look at a few of the many benefits of being in a relationship with someone who has ADHD. When using the Five Relationship Pillars, the benefits of ADHD shine bright.

Spontaneity

One of the benefits of having a weak working memory is the ability to be spontaneous. A weak working memory means not going through all the things that could go wrong or thinking through everything necessary before trying something new. Partners with ADHD can infuse life and energy in their relationships by being up for new things and prioritizing the moment rather than their to-do list. This is probably something that attracted you to your partner and is helpful in a relationship. After all, sometimes great things come from taking risks and being spontaneous!

Never-Say-Never Attitude

Because someone with ADHD tends to be hyperfocused and creative and loves a challenge, they know that they can accomplish anything if they put their minds to it. Figuring things out that no else can is a gift of ADHD. Hearing that it would be impossible activates the ADHD brain to figure out how to accomplish things and make everyone happy. Someone with ADHD will come up with a fun solution to make things happen that neurotypical brains wouldn't necessarily think of.

Hyperfocus

Due to their hyperfocus, adults with ADHD can produce and accomplish amazing things when they're interested in something. Many entrepreneurs and Olympic athletes, such as swimmer Michael Phelps, use their hyperfocus to be the best at what they do. This also comes in handy in times of a crisis as their brains can process a lot of information and organize it quickly.

Creativity

Because they are paying attention to everything, an adult with ADHD can take in a lot of information. This helps them think and process the world differently, which is commonly praised as creativity. They are idea generators, creators, and great problem solvers. It is a benefit to the relationship and to society. It can make them amazing parents as they can come up with fun games and capture kids' attention. This can make them highly successful in their careers. It can also keep their relationships novel and fun.

TIPS FOR SUCCESS

Hopefully the Five Relationship Pillars are ingrained in your memory by now. You know that using them as a foundation for everything you do can help your relationship be successful and fulfilling. Here are a few key reminders to help your neurodiverse relationship bloom.

Focus on the Five Relationship Pillars

Remember that the pillars can make the relationship a healthy and positive environment for both partners. Just like work, a toxic environment doesn't produce great workers and leaves employees feeling bitter, resentful, and unmotivated. A positive work environment has better results, even if an employee may need more training to be at their best. Focusing on the Five Relationship Pillars will allow each of you to be at your best and create a positive environment where both people are able to grow with support.

Focus on Treatment

If you are the partner with ADHD, mastering the right tools to help you work on strengthening your executive function skills and helpful habits will make your life easier in the long run. Yes, it may feel like rough seas at first, but it will be smoother sailing once you master these skills. Getting to know your brain is an investment in yourself. Information is power, and once you have it, you can make things work better for you. And if you picked up any of the common coping skills talked about in the book, like stressing out, treatment will help you learn strategies that help you without stress and anxiety. Treatment can be fun. I like to incorporate games and novel experiences that are helpful for adults with ADHD. Why? Because it is more effective! Remember, the non-ADHD partner can benefit from therapy as well. It can help them learn new skills and let go of resentments that negatively impact the relationship.

Medication

For those who have been diagnosed with ADHD, the right medication can be life changing. Medication can help with staying focused, which makes doing mundane tasks at home and at work so much easier. Medication doesn't work for everyone, but it does work for many. Medication can also decrease stressors in your life, allowing you more bandwidth to learn new skills in treatment. Medication with therapy is the most effective form of treatment, according to the Centers for Disease Control (CDC).

Division of Labor

Domestic partnerships require a teamwork approach. Do what workplaces do and work with your strengths within the relationship and assign each task. Adults with ADHD often do better with tasks that can become part of their daily routine (washing dishes, nightly pickup) or things that they find fun. Try to divide up responsibilities so that they are independent of each other. Knowing what each person is responsible for makes it easier for both partners to contribute equitably. Celebrations and rewards are key in helping the partner with ADHD learn new habits. Ultimately, they can contribute to the household without it hurting your relationship, when using the strategies in this book.

Education, Education, Education

There are so many great resources to get support and education around ADHD. *ADDitude Magazine* and podcast has great information and community support. "How to ADHD" is a great vlog with helpful tips. Educating yourself to better understand ADHD can help reduce the shame and common challenges people with ADHD face. The more knowledge you have, the more you can use it to your advantage. Having a reasonable expectation from your partner with ADHD will help you take care of yourself and the relationship. Expecting their brains to function like a neurotypical one will continually leave you frustrated.

Honest Communication

It's okay that things are hard. Many of these conflicts come from people trying to "help" their partner without actually talking to them about it. Taking a moment to figure out what is going on and checking in with your partner will give you both the information you need. For example, you may realize that things you are doing for your partner are not really helping them. Honest communication is necessary for the relationship pillar of acknowledgment. If you aren't truthful about how things affect you, your partner cannot acknowledge your effort or sacrifice if you don't share it with them.

Be Accountable

Being accountable for your part in a relationship is critical to the success of your relationship. It allows both partners to accurately acknowledge and discuss challenges, so that things can be better in the future. Without it, you would never be able to apologize or make a repair. Being accountable makes you a better person, not a failure. If each of you can celebrate accountability, you will be honoring your growth mindset. Being curious about what keeps you from being accountable will help you recognize what you need to feel safe and vulnerable in the relationship. Oftentimes, we don't acknowledge our blame because we don't want to believe that we could hurt our partner. But not being accountable is the thing that hurts your partner more.

Learn to Apologize

The most important thing in a relationship is not preventing a negative experience (they are inevitable) but knowing how to repair it. Being in a relationship means that you will disappoint someone, hurt someone, and mess up, and they will do the same to you. Knowing how to make it better is more important than not doing it in the first place, because that's nearly impossible. Getting good at being accountable, apologizing, and repairing will help your relationship and you in the long term. Apologizing is an investment in your relationship. Having a strong understanding of the pillar of positive acceptance can make it easier for you to apologize.

LIVING WITH ADHD

Your neurodiverse relationship can be amazing, supportive, and fulfilling, but you will still experience challenges and conflicts from time to time. It's important to be aware of when conflict might arise so that you can be sure to use the tools you've been learning. Such times include a job change or promotion, planning a wedding or another big celebratory event, having and raising kids, and taking care of a sick or aging parent. These times demand more executive functioning skills from both partners to manage more tasks. Fortunately, you are working on the skills that will help you avoid falling into negative cycles during these challenging times.

The Five Relationship Pillars—praise, acknowledgment, growth mindset, games, and positive acceptance—will fundamentally change your relationship and protect it from the toxicity that some couples experience. It also empowers both partners to focus on how they can add to the relationship to create a healthy environment instead of trying to change the other person in some way. Being able to positively accept someone for who they are is the greatest gift anyone could give to another. It is the foundation of safety, love, and security.

Know that you are not alone. Many neurodiverse couples have put in the work to overcome toxic cycles in their relationship with success. Getting support, sharing your story, and listening to other couples' stories can help you improve and deepen your relationship. Remember all the reasons you fell in love with your partner. Most likely, it was an epic love story and adventure. With the Five Relationship Pillars, it can be that again.

Resources

SUGGESTED READING

ADDitude Magazine: Inside the ADHD Mind
ADDitudeMag.com

Anita Robertson, LCSW: Adult Individual Therapy
StrengthInYourMind.com

Children and Adults with Attention-Deficit/Hyperactivity
Disorder (CHADD)
CHADD.org

The Couples Guide to Thriving with ADHD by Melissa Orlov and
Nancie Kohlenberger, LMFT (Specialty Press, Inc., 2014)

*Driven to Distraction: Recognizing and Coping with Attention Deficit
Disorder from Childhood through Adulthood* by Edward M. Hallowell,
MD, and John J. Ratey, MD (Anchor Books, 2011)

*Healing ADD: The Breakthrough Program that Allows You to See and
Heal the 7 Types of ADD* by Daniel G. Amen (Berkley Publishing
Group, 2013)

National Alliance on Mental Illness (NAMI)
NAMI also offers local support groups for individuals living with a
mental illness and loving someone with a mental illness.
NAMI.org

*Organizing Solutions for People with ADHD: Tips and Tools to Help You
Take Charge of Your Life and Get Organized* by Susan C. Pinsky (Fair
Winds Press, 2012)

The Smart but Scattered Guide to Success: How to Use Your Brain's Executive Skills to Keep Up, Stay Organized, and Get Organized at Work and at Home by Peg Dawson, EdD, and Richard Guare, PhD (Guilford Press, 2016)

INSPIRING PODCASTS

ADDitude Experts Podcast
ADDitudeMag.com/category/adhd-podcast

ADHD reWired by Eric Tivers
ADHDreWired.com

Distraction with Dr. Ned Hallowell
DistractionPodcast.com/category/episodes

VIDEOS

"How to ADHD" by Jessica McCabe on YouTube
YouTube.com/channel/UC-nPM1_kSZf91ZGkcgy_95Q

"Steep in Thought" by Anita Robertson and Jose Garcia on YouTube
YouTube.com/channel/UC4_HcWic7V3Ub3B74WMlFaA

HELPFUL APPS

Brili: Break down tasks, use timers, and get rewards
Brili.com

Clear: Tasks, reminders, and to-do lists

Countdown: Keep track of rewards and things to look forward to

Daylio: Tracks goals and mood

Focusmate: A virtual accountability/coworking buddy
Focusmate.com

Forest: Stay Focused: Productivity app

Headspace: Meditation and mindfulness app

Paprika: Keeps recipes and generates shopping lists
PaprikaApp.com

Trello: Task manager

PRODUCTIVITY PLANNERS

Hero's Journal: Uses a story to assist productivity, which can be helpful in changing a mundane task into something interesting for an ADHD brain.

Panda Planner: A planner that uses several strategies that are generally helpful to an ADHD brain.

References

Amen, Daniel. *Healing ADD: The Breakthrough Program That Allows You to See and Heal the 7 Types of ADD*. New York: The Berkley Publishing Group, 2013.

American Academy of Child & Adolescent Psychiatry. "ADHD & the Brain." February 2017. Accessed June 27, 2020. AACAP.org /AACAP/Families_and_Youth/Facts_for_Families/FFF-Guide /ADHD_and_the_Brain-121.aspx.

Barkley, Russell A. "Factsheets: What Causes ADHD?" Accessed June 27, 2020. RussellBarkley.org/factsheets/WhatCausesADHD2017.pdf.

Center for Disease Control and Prevention. "Data and Statistics about ADHD." CDC.gov. Last reviewed October 15, 2019. Accessed June 27, 2020. CDC.gov/ncbddd/adhd/data.html.

Dawson, Peg and Richard Guare. *The Smart but Scattered Guide to Success: How to Use Your Brain's Executive Skills to Keep Up, Stay Organized, and Get Organized at Work and at Home*. New York: Guilford Press, 2016.

Dodson, William. "ADHD and the Epidemic of Shame." *ADDitude Magazine*. Accessed June 27, 2020. ADDitudeMag.com/ slideshows/adhd-and-shame.

Fosco, Whitney D., Larry W. Hawk, Keri S. Rosch, and Michelle G. Bubnik. "Evaluating Cognitive and Motivational Accounts of Greater Reinforcement Effects among Children with Attention-Deficit/ Hyperactivity Disorder." *Behavioral and Brain Functions* 11, no. 20 (April 2015). doi.org/10.1186/s12993-015-0065-9.

Hallowell, Edward. "Hyperfocus: A Blessing and a Curse." ADDitude Magazine. Updated August 23, 2019. Accessed June 27, 2020. ADDitudeMag.com/adhd-symptoms-hyperfocus-attention.

Liddle, Elizabeth B., Chris Hollis, Martin J. Batty, Madeleine J. Groom, John J. Totman, Mario Liotti, Gaia Scerif, and Peter F. Liddle. "Task-Related Default Mode Network Modulation and Inhibitory Control in ADHD: Effects of Motivation and Methylphenidate." *Journal of Child Psychology and Psychiatry* 52, no. 7 (November 2010): 761–771. doi.org/10.1111/j.1469-7610.2010.02333.x.

Mohan, Akansha, Aaron J. Roberto, Abhishek Mohan, Aileen Lorenzo, Kathryn Jones, Martin J. Carney, Luis Liogier-Weyback, Soonjo Hwang, and Kyle A.B. Lapidus. "The Significance of the Default Mode Network (DMN) Neurological and Neuropsychiatric Disorders: A Review." *The Yale Journal of Biology and Medicine* 89, no. 1 (March 2016): 49–57. dash.harvard.edu/handle/1/26318604.

National Institutes of Health. "Dopamine Affects How Brain Decides Whether a Goal is Worth the Effort." NIH.gov. March 31, 2020. Accessed June 27, 2020. NIH.gov/news-events/nih-research -matters/dopamine-affects-how-brain-decides-whether-goal -worth-effort.

Orlov, Melissa. *The ADHD Effect on Marriage: Understand and Rebuild Your Relationship in Six Steps*. Plantation, Florida: Specialty Press, 2010.

Walkup, John T., Lauren Stossel, and Rebecca Rendelman. "Beyond Rising Rates: Personalized Medicine and Public Health Approaches to the Diagnosis and Treatment of Attention-Deficit/Hyperactivity Disorder." *Journal of the American Academy of Child & Adolescent Psychiatry* 53, 1 (January 2014): 14–16. doi.org/10.1016/j.jaac .2013.10.008.

Index

A

Accountability, 62, 70–71, 129, 134

Acknowledgment
  appreciation, showing for efforts
    made, 57, 58
  criticism filter, helping to
    decrease, 40
  examples of, 116
  honest communication as necessary
    for, 63, 129
  in I'll Grow with You exercise, 124
  importance of, 23, 79, 90, 105
  lack of, as harmful to a relationship,
    25, 29, 103
  as one of Five Relationship Pillars,
    17, 20, 56, 75, 80, 113, 130
  for organizing clutter, 87

ADDitude Magazine, 5, 8, 128, 132

ADHD brain
  adult ADHD diagnoses, 6–7, 14
  big rewards, as wired for, 5, 6, 10, 23
  clutter, as comfortable with, 31
  common issues with, 16
  criticism filter of, 8, 38, 39–40, 46
  different priorities of, 24, 34
  as easily distracted, 11, 30, 79, 82, 90
  executive functioning skills, as weak
    in, 13, 20, 29

hyperfocus abilities of, 5, 9–10,
    30, 57, 126
  intense feelings, as generating,
    12, 39, 61, 62
  neurological differences as affecting
    ability to focus, 25
  playful aspect to, 18
  praise as fuel for, 4, 6, 17
  stigma of ADHD, 112, 113
  stress, using as a tool to focus,
    42–43, 46
  upside of, 32, 44, 57, 81,
    92, 125–126
  weak attention skills of, 30
  weak emotional regulation
    of, 15
  See also Neurodiverse relationships

Apologizing, 62, 79, 106, 129

Apps, uses for, 52, 56, 57, 64,
    81, 134

Attention
  as an executive function skill,
    5, 11, 63
  anxiety, maintaining attention
    through, 38
  constant support and attention,
    ADHD brains needing, 43
  difficulty in sustaining, 14, 126

time management, impacting, 54

tip for refocusing attention, 53

weak attention skills, 16, 30, 74, 90

See also Praise

B

Barkley, Russell, 6

Biggest Fan technique, 100, 104

Boundaries, establishing, 68

Burnout of non-ADHD partners,
41–42, 46, 77, 82

C

Calendar sharing, 52, 57–58

Calm Down spaces, 64–65, 67

Check-ins, setting aside time for, 43, 46

Clean Sweep activity, 93

Clutter

ADHD, as linked with, 25,
31, 86, 89

executive functions needed to
clear, 90–91

growing up in clutter, 87

in There Is Help activity, 119

visual reminder, using as, 94

Conflict cycle, example of, 15

Copy That! strategy, 80

Co-regulation of emotions, 69

Couples therapy, 117–118

Criticism

clarification, asking for, 41

criticism filter, 38, 40, 46, 67

hyper sensitivity to, 8–9, 24, 39, 78

imagined criticism, 42–43

as negative reinforcement, 92

in There Is Help activity, 119

toxic environment, creating with,
25, 29–30

D

Daily affirmations, 101

Dawson, Peg, 7

Default mode network (DMN),
5–6, 17, 51

Deflate Your Emotional Balloon
exercise, 65

Distraction

ADHD brain as easily distracted, 11,
30, 79, 82, 90

apps, using to refocus, 56

hyperfocus without distraction, 10

mundane tasks, distraction
during, 14

in There Is Help activity, 119

time management challenges, 49

during transition between tasks,
50, 53, 58

weak executive functions and, 51

See also Focus

Dodson, William, 8

Dopamine, 5, 17, 50, 51

Downtime activities, 53

Dweck, Carol, 18

Dyslexia as an example of
neurodiversity, 3, 4

E

Emotional regulation, 12, 15, 63, 64,
68–69, 71, 119

Executive functions

ADHD brain, weaker executive
function skills of, 13, 20, 29

adulting, executive function skills as
necessary for, 7–8, 13

brakes, picturing executive function
skills as, 5, 9, 71

during challenging times, 130

G

Games
  ADHD brains as thriving
    with, 18, 20
  benefits of playing, 17, 63, 127
  creativity, expressing through, 126
  criticism, filter, decreasing
    through, 40
  distraction, avoiding with, 30
  game playing as a downtime
    activity, 53
  harm of neglecting, 25, 103
  in I'll Grow with You exercise, 125
  making space for, 113
  as one of Five Relationship
    Pillars, 130
  Relationship Connection
    game, 106–107
  tidying the home, making into a
    game, 94
Genetic component to ADHD, 6, 7, 87
Get Specific strategy, 32
Get the Facts! strategy, 41
Growth mindset
  accountability as a part of, 129
  checklists, applying during
    creation of, 55
  communication through, 32
  criticism filter, helping to
    decrease, 40
  defining, 18
  example of, 116
  in I'll Grow with You exercise, 125
  lack of as harmful, 25, 103
  as one of Five Relationship Pillars,
    17, 20, 113, 130

  sharing of feelings under, 63
  in therapy, 117
  in There Is Help activity, 118
Guare, Richard, 7

H

Hallowell, Edward, 5, 9

I

"I Failed" strategy, 40–41
"I" statements, 30–31, 54, 65,
    70, 71, 79
I'll Grow with You exercise, 124–125

K

Keep It Simple strategy, 88

L

Labeled Bins technique, 92
Lists as management tools, 55–56, 58,
    100, 104, 114–115

M

Medication
  as an option, 127–128
  fear of taking, 112
  in Pair Your Activities technique, 76
  remembering to take as a
    challenge, 75
  Ritalin, 5–6
  in There Is Help activity,
    120, 127–128
  treatment choices, respecting,
    113, 121
Mindfulness activities, 64, 65, 134
Miscommunication, avoiding, 80
Moods, 58, 80, 115, 134

Orlov, Melissa, 116
Overfunctioning, 77, 78, 102, 103, 108, 119

P

Pair Your Activities strategy, 76
Parent-child dynamic, 97, 100, 101, 108
Positive acceptance
    apologizing, importance to a relationship, 129
    boundaries, establishing, 68
    challenges of maintaining, 67, 103
    in Co-Regulation exercise, 69
    criticism filter, as helping to decrease, 40
    defining, 18–19
    example of, 116
    in I'll Grow with You exercise, 125
    in Independence strategy, 55, 56–57
    as one of Five Relationship Pillars, 17, 20, 75, 90, 113, 130
    sharing feelings, ease of, 63
Positive reinforcement, 4, 25, 34, 57, 58, 93, 100
Praise
    ADHD brain as motivated by, 10, 17, 20, 94
    changes in ADHD brain, as causing, 6, 17
    consistency, need for, 19
    criticism filter, helping to decrease, 40
    growth mindset, as part of, 55
    in I'll Grow with You exercise, 124
    importance of, 79, 87, 90, 130
    neglecting to praise, harmful effects of, 25, 30, 103

as positive feedback, 58, 63
positive reinforcement, as a type of, 4, 80, 113
as a strategy, 91–92, 100
tips on nurturing praise and acknowledgment, 57, 81, 116
Productivity planners, 52, 134

R

Reinforcement
    of a desired action, 81
    of executive function skills, 7
    negative reinforcement, 4, 92, 99, 108
    positive reinforcement, 4, 25, 34, 57, 58, 93, 100
    visual reminders, pairing with reinforcement, 76
Relationship Connection game, 106–107
Reminders
    Calm Down Space, visual reminders in, 64
    "change oil" car icon as an example of, 104
    clutter, using as a visual reminder, 85, 87
    daily reminders, setting on phone, 33
    as feedback, 68
    in I'll Grow with You activity, 125
    importance of, 52, 58
    key holders, putting by the door as a reminder, 88
    labeled bins as visual reminders, 92
    miscommunication, avoiding, 80
    natural reminders, use of timers when absent, 53
    shared calendar, effectiveness of, 57

Acknowledgments

I am grateful to the staff at Callisto Media for the opportunity to write this book. Meera Pal and Joe Cho were a pleasure to work with, and I'm particularly thankful for Meera's enthusiasm and support. I am especially grateful for my husband, who took on more parenting and household responsibilities during a pandemic so that I could write this book.

About the Author

Anita Robertson, LCSW, is a psychotherapist in Austin, Texas. She works with individuals and couples with ADHD. She runs an ADHD Relationship Bootcamp for couples who want to learn the necessary skills to enjoy the benefits of their neurodiverse relationship while avoiding common conflicts. Anita advocates for mental health access and resources for her community. She normalizes talking about mental health as a co-vlogger at the Steep in Thought YouTube channel, and provides tips and information about common relationship issues on her blog at AnitaRobertson.com.